Also By Randy Elrod

The Loss of Belonging

Ten Steps to A New (and Better) Tribe

Randy Elrod

Contact The Author

To book Randy Elrod for speaking or a
Mandala Workshop
Email: randy@randyelrod.com

For more information: www.randyelrod.com

cre:ate 2.0
Publishing

Bulk purchase and reprint permission may be requested from randy@randyelrod.com

Printed in the United States of America

Library of Congress Cataloging-in-Publication Data has been applied for.

ISBN # 978-0-9914715-5-3

To Gina

A companion who knows
who I am and loves me anyway.
I have found myself in you.

Contents

Introduction

> Everything I cared about was gone,
> and it hurts so badly.
> But why would I want that feeling to go away?
> The pain, their loss, it's all I have left of them.
> You think the grief will make you smaller inside,
> like your heart will collapse in on itself.
> But it doesn't.
> I feel spaces opening up inside of me,
> like a building with rooms, I've never explored.

Dolores Abernathy (Westworld)

B elonging means fitting in with others and feeling like an accepted member of a group. When we talk about the value of a tribe, we imply that sense of belonging. It is something all of us need and long for, and it is primal and fundamental to our understanding of happiness and well-being.

It is in close personal relationships—where we work, play, live, and worship—that we find our most intense belonging. But it's also the place where our dark sides find expression. Because our tribe has such a significant effect on us—when it is dysfunctional and mobilized in negative ways—it wields great power.

In the early 2000s, I experienced the loss of belonging. I lost my tribe—most of my fans, acquaintances, friends, family, and companions. My social networks and the business which provided my income became a barren wasteland. What once felt like a vibrant tribe of people—left me with almost no friends or natural support system. Some of them say I abandoned them, and perhaps they are right. After all, I had sinned.

In 2006, I resigned my thirty-year career while wrestling with an existential crisis. Most of my life had been geared toward achieving material success, but after attaining it, the hollowness in my being was painfully apparent. I was empty.

A few isolated months later I stumbled into a brief affair which left my marriage of twenty-seven years in confusion. Tormented by guilt, I soon confessed and asked forgiveness, but my wife was gravely wounded and could not reconcile my transgression. Our Christian ideals led us to cling to the scuppered marriage so long as no one mentioned the adulterous truth. We both drowned in private shame, slowly suffocating for five lovelorn years.

In 2011, a long-time friend who had recently gone through a divorce (and with whom I had enjoyed a twenty-year platonic connection) began to resuscitate my asphyxiated being. The relationship gradually blossomed, and we fell in love.

But the affair scandalized our Bible Belt community, who saw the liaison as evidence of debauchery, which justified their shaming, condemning, and ostracizing—all sanctioned in the holy name of religion.

I would walk down the streets of our dystopian evangelical town, and the people would coldly turn their heads. They would silently go to the other side of the road and act as if I did not exist. I was invisible. I no longer belonged to their kind. I had been caught in adultery, and far too proper to cast stones, they piously declared me unfit and dead to their world. For a human being to be rendered invisible is worse than being condemned.

Together we fled the cliquish small town for the anonymity of a metropolitan city far away—in hopes of finding a sense of belonging once again. After a time of grieving, we timidly embarked upon the search for a new and better tribe.

Paradoxically, as time passed, my former tribe began to realize much to their dismay that their estrangement led me to what turned out to be a much happier and prosperous life. A past due divorce granted me freedom, and my friend and I eventually married. I had found a companion who accepts me for the person I am becoming, and who celebrates my questions and uncertainty about the mystery of existence.

To this day, almost a decade later, I have been abandoned by my nuclear family, former pastors, thousands of members of the churches I had served faithfully, by tens of thousands in my social networks, and all but a handful of my closest friends

Their psychosis had turned adoration and admiration into hatred and loathing. I had lost my tribe—my sense of belonging.

Benjamin Corey calls it *ghosting* in his insightful blog post. He says ghosting "is when someone abruptly ends a friendship with limited or no explanation, and when they proceed to disappear from your life quickly. They ghost people. They disappear from our lives. They abandon us. They sever ties. And they do it in the cruelest way possible: with silence."

He goes on to say, "I don't think they realize that on the day they ghosted me, it was the day that my life started to seriously unravel. No one cared if I survived as a person. Every waking morning was a reminder that none of them gave a shit about me. I don't think they realize that years later, the idea of going to church again or having Christian friends I can trust, is outside of what would be healthy or plausible for me."

"I don't think they realize that when they see us at the department store and turn to walk away before we see them, they're not quick enough. I don't think they realize that I never fully recovered from that life event and that it still impacts me on a daily basis. I felt it yesterday, I feel it today, and I fear I'll feel it tomorrow, too. I don't think they realize any of those things. Sadly I don't think they care, either—because if they did, they would have attempted to bind up the wounds they inflicted without letting so many years go by."[1]

These are heart-rending words that sound eerily familiar uttered by someone who has experienced a destructive loss of belonging. It's not only Benjamin Corey and myself; unfortunately, the ranks of the "ghosted" are growing at an alarming rate. We are all struggling in one way or another.

How does one survive the loss of their tribe? After all, a sense of belonging is a basic human need, like the need for food and shelter. To belong means to be accepted as a member or part of something important. Perhaps we can glean encouragement from Ralph Waldo Emerson in his essay *Compensation* when he promises that "every evil to which we do not succumb is a benefactor." He goes on, "What does not kill us, makes us stronger."[2]

Eight difficult years after being ghosted by the majority of my tribe, the following chapters highlight ten steps that helped me survive, and to employ an overused cliché, to thrive. The first two steps will help you gain a new urgency about the importance of finding healing. They deal with grief, loss, and betrayal. The passage about forgiveness, the most neglected aspect of the healing arts, provides a springboard for a sense of meaning in your personal life.

The next four steps are guides to a path toward becoming who you are—to understanding a sense of self. These guideposts will help open up essential spaces inside of you, like a building with rooms you've never explored. You will look at the fascinating true story of a small town which proves that those of us who feel life has meaning and purpose are more likely to be in good physical and psychological health.

The final three steps (along with a bonus section of 17 additional steps) show that when you find a tribe—when you experience a sense of place—it improves your motivation, health, and happiness. Finding others also helps you understand that everyone struggles and goes through difficult times. This will help you feel less alone.

Tribal relationships are vital to all of us, but we live in a society where the importance of camaraderie is undervalued. Indeed, most of our news and social media seem keen to emphasize what divides us instead of what brings us together. This means it is up to each of us to build a sense of self and wholeness and to fully experience a sense of others. Achieving this might not be easy. However, if it leads to a life of meaning and purpose, and if it improves our health and well-being, it is worth the effort.

Several chapters conclude with vital questions to ask yourself. They are not exhaustive, but I hope these ten steps will serve as the beginning of your journey to regain belonging and to find a new and better tribe. It is not an easy road, but the adventure will prove life-transforming.

This book shows that loss can ultimately be a positive thing. The displacement of the noise of my tribe has led to solitude, healing, self-acceptance, and wholeness. The refutation of control wielded by the institutions of life has given me freedom. The escape from mindless teaching has encouraged an insatiable curiosity. The liberation of sexual repression has blossomed to a sensual awakening, and the renunciation of self-denial and shame has promoted intimacy and communion.

Has it been easy? No. Has it been worth it? Yes. A resounding yes! Never in my life has there been a time when I learned so much about myself, the world, and others.

The words of psychologist James Hollis, sociologist Joseph Campbell, philosopher Jean-Claude Sartre, and many others have inspired and given me the courage to write these words. They teach that we must free ourselves from the chains forged by the institutions of life—family, religion, education, society—and connect with our passion, or in the words of Campbell, to "follow our bliss."

Unfortunately, that often means ghosting, suffering, and loss. But the words of these wise men and the hard lessons gleaned from my experience teach that we do not have to fear the loss of belonging. They have shown me the only real fear in life is dying having never lived. We need to learn to live our lives, and we must find a tribe to share our experiences with.

These men have prompted this writer to encourage others by detailing my quest and taught me that that which pulls us into the crucible, is the thing that can transform us, and lead us into our true being. This book comes from the center of my person. The reason for my existence is to encourage others.

I invite you to join me on this hope-filled quest. There are more than a few steps to anything in this messy reality called life, but my objective is that the following pages will clear the path to find healing, find you, and then find others—a new (and better) tribe.

I. Finding Healing

Step 1

In Which We Seek To Understand Grief and Loss

This is a book about hope. The title seems to belie that fact and the words of the first step could make it sound even more suspicious. But you will soon find that hope permeates this journey of words and images. In the words of Andy Dufresne in the movie *Shawshank Redemption*, "Hope is a good thing, maybe even the best of things, and good things never die."[3]

Grief and loss are inevitable in the natural order of things. But it's the hope that happens *after* the loss that counts.

If you are reading this, you are perhaps all too familiar with grief, loss, or betrayal. But most of us are *not* acquainted with the healing comfort that can be found within our self. We have bought into the deception and despair of self-denial, and we administer kindness to everyone but ourselves.

As a child, I was taught an acrostic in Sunday School. JOY—Jesus, Others, You. It took me forty-three years of life to realize that seemingly innocent play on words was a debilitating lie. We see this deception exposed in (of all places) the Hebrew Bible. Jesus Christ taught the opposite principle in what he called the greatest commandment. He said, "Love others *as you love yourself.*"[4]

The prerequisite to loving others is loving our self. We must learn to love ourselves, and only *then* will we be able to cherish others. For many of us, this flies in the face of our religious upbringing.

JOY is an acronym for hopelessness. I propose three different letters. HYO—Healing, You, and Others. An acrostic of hope. Admittedly, it's not as catchy, but HYO is the goal of this book. Finding Healing, Finding You, and Finding Others.

The hope of finding a new (and better) tribe is possible *after* we find healing and after we find ourselves. Let's gather our courage and get started.

At first, I questioned including chapters addressing the topics of grief, loss, and betrayal. There has been so much written about this subject matter that it seemed unnecessary and redundant.

But as I talked with people who have experienced the loss of belonging, a recurring theme emerged. Even though they were familiar with the terms—the hectic pace of life had induced most of them to sweep these painful emotions under the rug of workaholism, alcoholism, church attendance, or other activities and never wrestle with them.

The catastrophic events surrounding my existential crisis—a divorce, estrangement from my children, shame from my former tribe, and relocation to an unfamiliar place were overwhelming. I tried to ignore my sadness and drown it out with day to day existence. Finally, I sat down with a person who had been highly recommended as an adviser.

We talked for several hours, and to this day, one question sticks out from that emotionally charged conversation. He asked, "Have you taken time to grieve your loss of belonging?"

My sorrow was such that he thought it vital for me to consult a trained counselor. I will talk more about this in Step #3. The critical issue at hand is that working through these emotions is a necessary step to finding a new (and better) tribe.

Grief and loss are central parts of human existence. Our lives start and finish with a loss. Along the journey, there are multiple losses—of self, of innocence, of connectedness, and of friends and companions. If we live to old age, we will lose everyone we care about. If we do not live long enough, they will have forgotten us.

The poet Rilke says it this way, "So we live, forever saying farewell."[5] That's depressing. Fortunately, another poet provides words of encouragement. Alfred Lord Tennyson writes, "It is better to have loved and lost than not to have loved at all."[6]

In 1969, psychiatrist Elisabeth Kübler-Ross introduced what became known as the *five stages of grief.* They were based on her studies of the feelings of patients facing a terminal illness, but they apply to other types of adverse life changes and losses. In many ways, a loss of belonging can be more painful than death because the parties involved are still alive and there is no benefit of closure.

The five stages of grief:
1. Denial
2. Anger
3. Bargaining
4. Depression
5. Acceptance

Dr. Kübler-Ross hastens to say, "You do not have to go through each stage to heal. Some people resolve their grief without going through any of these stages. If you do go through the stages, you probably won't experience them in neat, sequential order. So don't worry about what you 'should' be feeling or which stage you're supposed to be in."[7]

She never intended these stages be a rigid framework that applies to everyone who mourns. In her final book, she said of the five stages of grief: "They were never meant to help tuck messy emotions into neat packages. They are responses to loss that many people have, but there is not a typical response to loss, as there is no typical loss. Our grieving is as individual as our lives."[8]

As I wrestled with the question that was posed to me by the adviser ("Have you taken time to grieve your loss?"), it was soon apparent that I was stuck in the first two stages of grief—denial and anger. This awareness helped me progress to the next steps in the healing process. I slowly began to see the light at the end of the darkness.

Hospice Foundation of America likens grief to a roller coaster. "Instead of a series of stages, we might think of the grieving process as full of ups and downs, highs and lows. Like many roller coasters, the ride tends to be rougher in the beginning so the initial valleys may be deeper and longer."[9]

"The problematic periods should become less intense and shorter as time goes by. But it takes time to work through these emotions. Even years after a loss, at special events or holidays, such as a family wedding, the birth of a child, and Christmas time, we may still experience a strong sense of grief."[10]

The birth and death life-cycle of interpersonal relationships is a regular and recurring part of life.

Psychologist George Levinger, in his *ABCDE model*, says the natural development of a relationship follows five stages:

1. Acquaintance: Becoming acquainted depends on many factors including, proximity, first impressions, attractiveness, similarities in personality, attitude, and interests and association to favorable situations. Acquaintance may lead to the next stage or can continue indefinitely.

2. Build up: Beginning to trust and care about each other. Here there is a need for compatibility and filtering agents such as common background, cultural background, and related interests. Compatibility will influence whether or not interaction continues.

3. Continuation: Following a mutual commitment to long-term relationships this is generally a long and relatively stable period. Continued growth and development will occur during this time.

4. Deterioration: Relationships deteriorate as a result of boredom, resentment, and dissatisfaction. Individuals may communicate less and avoid self-disclosure. Loss and betrayals may take place continuing the downward spiral.

5. Ending: This marks the end of the relationship by complete termination or separation.[11]

Ending a relationship and losing someone you love and care deeply about is very painful. You may experience all kinds of complicated feelings, and it may seem like the pain and sadness will never let up. These are normal reactions to a significant loss. Prolonged sorrow can be an indicator to take care of yourself. While there is no right or wrong way to grieve, there are healthy ways to cope with the pain that, in time, can *renew* you and permit you to move on.[12]

Grief is a natural and honest response to a loss of belonging. Especially the deprivation of something we greatly value. Emotional suffering occurs when someone you love is taken away, and the more significant the loss, the more intense the grief will be. But take a moment and listen to these words of hope. *The intensity of your emotions says a beautiful thing about you—you can feel deeply.*

Psychologist Marilyn Winell explains, "You could be very angry. While some people find ways to express themselves during this phase, most wonder what to do with all their anger. Because of past religious teachings, you might think that you should just forgive and forget rather than accept these feelings as legitimate."

"The rage may then go underground and stay with you. Bottled up emotions like these can leave you feeling hopeless, helpless, anxious, and depressed." She goes on to say, "If you have left your religion, the loss of relationship with God can feel devastating, as though your parents have died; you no longer have a Heavenly Father. The losses are multiple—a primary love relationship with the divine, a spiritual family, and a supportive community."[13]

We do not have to be enslaved to the loss, but an active participant in the act of letting go.[14] The experience of displacement can only be acute when we have lost something of value that has been in our life. If there is no experience of loss, there was nothing of value.

To find healing, we are required to acknowledge, and as we shall see later in Step #9, to celebrate the value, we have been given. Our job is to discern the worth we have been granted and to acknowledge it even when we can no longer personally attach to that person who gave rise to it.

We never lose those we love. Nothing which is internalized is ever lost. Even in the grief something valuable remains. In the Jewish faith, the "unveiling" of the gravestone on the first anniversary of death is a dual acknowledgment of the gravity of loss and a reminder of the end of grieving so that life might renew itself.

The circle of life—the rhythm of gain and loss—is outside our control and what remains within our command is the attitude of willingness to find in even the bitterest losses what remains to be lived.

Grieving is a very personal experience. How you grieve depends on many factors, including your personality and coping style, your life experience, your faith, and the nature of the loss.[15]

The grieving process takes time. Healing happens gradually; it can't be forced or hurried, and there is no "normal" timetable. Some people start to feel better in weeks or months. For others, the grieving process is measured in years.[16]

Uncovering and grieving the loss of belonging will be crucial in releasing you from your pain. Remember, this process is similar to recovering from the death of a loved one. Whatever your grief experience, it's essential to be patient with yourself and allow the process to unfold naturally.[17]

The single most important factor in healing from loss is having the support of other people.[18] Even if you aren't comfortable talking about your feelings under normal circumstances, it's crucial to express them when you're grieving. Sharing your loss with trustworthy people makes the burden of grief more manageable to carry. Wherever the support originates, accept it and do not grieve alone. Connecting to others will help you heal.

If available, turn to friends and family members or draw comfort from your religion. Others have found help by joining a support organization such as a grief recovery group. Reputable organizations can be found online, and their goal is to assist people in taking effective action to recover from the emotional pain of loss.

If you do not have any of these options available and the grief is unbearable, call an experienced therapist. The loss of family, tribe, or community can be cataclysmic. Like an orphan child, you no longer have that circle of familiarity and safety. My therapist was invaluable in helping me grieve heartbreaking losses: the loss of my marriage, children, grandchildren, religious community, career, and most of my friends.

Some additional ways to express your grief are:

1) Write a letter to say farewell to your lost tribe, to God, or to your family, that is intended for your eyes only. Be honest. Let the emotion flow. Being angry is okay.

2) The Native American culture has a "fire ceremony," in which you write your loss on a piece of paper, burn it in a sacred fire, and then let it go to the heavens.[19]

3) Try art therapy, expressing your sadness through art. Classes are available for all levels of experience.

Psychologist J. William Worden provides five critical questions to ask ourselves when dealing with grief:

1) Am I ready to accept the reality of the loss?

2) Am I ready to experience the pain of grief?

3) Have I adjusted to an environment in which the lost one(s) are missing?

4) Have I begun to invest in a loving relationship with myself?

5) Have I reinvested emotional energy into another relationship?

Do your best to answer these crucial questions honestly. Take time with them. Go over them with a trusted friend, at a support group, or with your therapist. Remember, the most critical factor in healing from loss is having the support of other people.

The rhythm of gain and loss is outside our control; what continues within our control is the willingness to find in even the bitterest losses that which remains to be lived. There is hope. You can recover and find a new and better tribe.

Step 2

In Which We Seek To Understand Betrayal and Forgiveness

B etrayal is a form of loss—a loss of innocence, trust, and relationship. And it's much easier to forgive deception by an enemy than a friend. If you have been betrayed (and who hasn't), then it is difficult to trust. We must not let the past wounds of disloyalty dominate our choices in the present, or we will be defined by days gone by.

Somehow we must find the capacity to forgive betrayal. The ability to forgive is not only a recognition of our own tendency to betray; it is the only move that can free us from the shackles of the past.

There is hope—good can come from treachery. Betrayal allows us to know and identify our real friends. Our true friends are those who love us for *who we are*. Our false friends are those who love us for *what we can do for them*.

Betrayal can simplify our life. Having a smaller number of friends gives us time and energy to devote to those connections. Having a large tribe deprives us of the time to invest deeply into each relationship.

If that is true, why does betrayal hurt so much? Lewis Smedes says in his insightful book, *The Art of Forgiveness*, "One of God's better jokes on us was to give us the power to remember the past and leave us no power to undo it."[20]

We can experience shunning by those we trust most. Perhaps you are walking down the street and see a friend who strolls by as if you did not exist. It doesn't matter that the friend was preoccupied and did not see you.

Momentarily you are less your self than before. The effect is similar to being asked why you look so rough today. No matter what loving concern may be motivating the compassionate inquiry, suddenly you feel robbed of a piece of your self-image, of a confirming response to your presence. Self-psychology and psychologists such as Heinz Kohut[21] would conceptualize that the missing or faulty reply is equivalent to a loss of a part of yourself.

Unfortunately, our communities often exhibit this sort of behavior to former tribe members who have embarrassed them by their mistakes. They believe these traitors are a blight and should be judged accordingly. The shunning action is justified with terms and excuses like "tough love," "you left us because you were not one of us," "I may forgive, but I won't forget," and "shame on you!"

In today's world, the transgressor is ostracized (ghosted) in both the physical world and the digital world of social networks. It's as though you do not exist. In essence, the former tribe strips you of your self-worth and your self-image. To understand and forgive this sort of betrayal is very difficult.

During the darkest days of my life, I was dealing with divorce and reeling from a community of "friends" that had shamed and subsequently shunned me. While trying to salvage the business I had built entirely with conservative Christian clients, I was told a former co-worker had formed a company identical to mine, in the same town, and had used my mailing list to recruit the tribe I had worked for twelve years to build.

To add further injury, this was someone I had repeatedly defended and protected from termination by our former boss. I had provided a recommendation that had assured his new job. He had been a protégé, and I could not believe the betrayal.

After I had worked through the fog of my own mistakes, his face kept recurring as one of the places of deep hurt I had not resolved. To this day, that person does not believe he was wrong and has not asked forgiveness. I discussed this with my therapist and told him the story in detail. He was able to provide valuable guidance.

When I relocated away from my therapist, meditation walks were helpful in my continued recovery from betrayal and the loss of my tribe. Walking meditation is an age-old practice that is about awareness and purification. It takes an everyday activity—walking—and raises it, elevating it from the physical realm to the emotional and spiritual.

Author Eric Weiner inspired my healing jaunts in his thought-provoking *Man Seeks God.* In the book, he describes a walking meditation guided by a Kabbalah teacher.[22] (Read about it in detail by following the endnote.)

Kabbalah is a mystical philosophy of Jewish meditation. You may be vaguely familiar with it because the pop star Madonna was famously involved with the movement during the 1990s.

Four in 10 American adults now say they meditate at least weekly.[23] What's different—and perhaps comforting—about Eastern religions is that they are existing schools of thought practiced by over a billion people. Because relatively few Caucasian Americans grew up in these religions, they generally don't associate any baggage with it like some do with the Christianity of their childhoods.

Buddhist nun Pema Chodron has an aphorism that says "everything is workable."[24] This means, essentially, that something positive can come out of even the most heartbreaking moments.

According to Buddhism, there are two possible reasons someone might cause us harm: It's their character to be hurtful, or second, a temporary situation caused them to act in a damaging way. Either way, it doesn't make sense to be bitter at the person. The nature of mud is dirt, but you wouldn't rage at the earth for getting you dirty. And you wouldn't curse the clouds for having a weather pattern that caused the mud.

Some people utilize Buddhist beliefs in conjunction with therapists who incorporate Eastern philosophy into their practices. "There's an overlap between the reason people will come to therapy and the reason they come to meditation," says Hugh Byrne, the director of the *Center for Mindful Living* in Washington, D.C.[25]

It is challenging to forgive betrayal, especially that which seems deliberate. This statement bears repeating: the willingness to forgive is not only a recognition of our own capacity to betray, but it is the only move which can ultimately free us from the shackles of the past.

How often do we see embittered souls with hard faces, still unforgiving of the former spouse or friend who betrayed them? They are, through their enslavement of the past, still chained to the betrayer, defined and corroded by the acid of hate. I have also seen divorced persons who carry a hatred of former spouses for years— and some, for a lifetime.

We must let go of resentments. Grudges harm every aspect of our being. Bitterness feels like we are holding on to a lump of hot coal and yet complaining that it's burning us.

"We attach our feelings to the moment when we were hurt, endowing it with immortality. And we let it assault us every time it comes to mind. It travels with us, sleeps with us, hovers over us while we make love, and broods over us while we die. Our hate does not even have the decency to die when those we hate pass away—for it is a parasite sucking OUR blood, not theirs. There is only one remedy for it—forgiveness."[26]

A release of these bitter emotions is what makes forgiveness healing. That's why forgiveness could be called the most neglected of the healing arts.

We fight wars, we kill each other, we harbor prejudice, and families refuse to speak to each other. All because we do not practice the art of forgiveness. Forgiveness provides the means to recover from the wounds of yesterday that should never have been.

We must realize that happiness is not the best revenge—forgiveness is. Revenge constricts rather than enlarges our being and binds us to days gone by. Those consumed by hate, no matter how legitimate their grievance, remain victims.

Dr. Lewis Smedes says, "No one is a professional at forgiving. We are all amateurs and bunglers. Be patient with yourself. Make the first step. Here are five things about forgiving somebody who wronged you."[27]

1. Forgiving is the only way to be fair to yourself after someone hurts you unfairly.

2. Forgivers are not doormats; they do not have to tolerate the bad things that they forgive.

3. Forgivers are not fools; they forgive and heal themselves, but they do not have to go back for more abuse.

4. We don't have to wait until the other person atones before we forgive them and heal ourselves.

5. Forgiving is a journey. It takes time, be patient and don't get discouraged if you lapse and have to do it over again.

Smedes continues, "The first person who gets the benefit of forgiving is always the person who does the forgiving. When you forgive a person who wronged you, you set a prisoner free, and then you discover that the prisoner you set free is you."

"When you forgive, you heal the hurts you should never have felt in the first place. Most people who cannot forgive a person who betrayed them handicap themselves by a mistaken understanding of what forgiving is."

He identifies three stages of the art of forgiving:

1) Restoring humanity to the person who betrayed us.

2) Surrendering our right to get even.

3) Beginning to bless the person we forgive.

If we can practice the art of forgiveness, and face these challenges internally, we will have a much broader sense of our inner self. We will then be able to say, "Ah, here is another thing I did not know about myself."

The rhythm of gain and loss is outside our control; what continues within our control is the attitude to find in even the bitterest losses what remains to be lived. Forgiveness gives birth to hope for the future.

Acts of betrayal urge many hard questions:

- "What sort of things should we forgive?"

- "How do I forgive someone who has not asked for forgiveness?"

- "Does forgiveness obligate me to renew our friendship?"

- "Does forgiveness mean restoration?"

Our personal acts of betrayal cause many difficult questions as well:

- "How do I forgive myself?"

- "How do I forgive those who exiled me?"

- "How do I forgive God?"

I have found Lewis Smedes book *The Art of Forgiving*[28] to be an invaluable resource. It is a Christian-centric book, but it contains practical truths and insights for anyone who has suffered betrayal and loss.

If you've experienced a loss of belonging, for whatever reason, it is better to find a way to heal the wounds of betrayal, to practice the art of forgiveness, and to maintain the hope that other people share your need for intimacy and closeness. You can trust again. You can find a new and better tribe.

The Loss of Belonging: Ten Steps To A New (& Better) Tribe

Step 3

In Which We Seek To Understand Counseling and Therapists

Not everyone needs therapy, but I tell my story to stress how invaluable treatment was to me in finding help. The loss of belonging is one of the most unfortunate tragedies that can happen to a human being.

The day after my world came crashing down a highly respected friend and confidant recommended a therapist in my local area of Franklin, Tennessee. It was crucial that the therapist was certified and well-trained since much of my carnage at that time resulted from seeing an unlicensed "life-coach/counselor" from my former church.

But unfortunately, this was to be yet another lousy therapy experience. The Franklin psychologist and I were oil and water. He was aloof and abrupt (which I'm sure suited my CEO friend who had recommended him) and utilized the opposite style I needed to find the vulnerability to open up my wounded soul.

At the end of our third horrific session, I stumbled out to my Jeep Wrangler, and with tears of despair filling my eyes, I searched for the keys stowed under the emergency brake. Through my haze, I dropped them deep into the narrow metal opening that housed the brake handle. It was like a game I played as a child, trying to grab a large handful of pennies from a jar, not wanting to open my fist, but unable to get them out. In my desperation to fish the keys out of the crevice and get away from there, I sliced my wrist deeply.

It was a fitting metaphor for how therapy was working out for me thus far in life. To this day I have a scar that looks as though I attempted suicide by slitting my wrist. At the next session, I terminated the destructive relationship—still devastated from the sudden loss of my friends, family, and my home.

This was the backstory to my first session a year later with Dr. Steve. I found myself sitting in unfamiliar surroundings at a coffee shop on 2nd and Congress in faraway Austin, Texas. It was like an out of body experience —exposing my heart to a stranger through the recommendation of a friend. Fortunately, he was well-versed and experienced in what he termed "the barren wasteland of therapy" permeating that Texas city. He gently recommended a professional to guide me through the stages of grief and recovery.

I called the counselor immediately, left a voicemail, and waited. A few hours later, Dr. Steve (he requested that I respect his privacy by using only his first name in my public writings) returned my call, and we set up an interview session. As is the case for most good therapists he was fully booked and his hourly (in reality the meetings were only 50 minutes) fee was significant. Intuitively I realized this may be one of the most important decisions of my life and we were finally able to work out a solution. I "borrowed" the money from my retirement savings knowing I was investing in my self—my health and recovery—without which there would be no need for an annuity.

Dr. Steve and I saw each other weekly (and in rare cases bi-weekly) for almost two years. Every minute spent in the sessions and every dollar invested was worth it. The psychotherapy helped me find my self and laid the foundation for taking the next steps in finding a new and better tribe. Here are a few personal insights about my various therapy experiences before we look at questions to ask when getting help.

Before the initial meeting, I meticulously researched steps in finding the right therapist, and this time I prepared a list of questions and concerns. It is crucial (and easy to forget) during intense suffering that the client paying the bill is the one that should determine the parameters and direction for the counseling relationship.

To my surprise, he appreciated and welcomed my interrogation, and voiced the importance that both of us feel good about the interaction and the chemistry between us. It was a mutual interview at no charge. The compatibility between us was unlike anything I had experienced previously in therapy. Dr. Steve was thoroughly professional but highly empathic. He was friendly, curious, and intelligent.

Several aspects of the next two years are worth mentioning. Each minute with Dr. Steve cost approximately four dollars. To put this in perspective, this was more than the extravagant hourly fee I paid my divorce attorney. Since I was sacrificing a great deal to afford this treatment, I felt it my responsibility to be thoroughly prepared for each session. I would have copious notes from the previous meetings and detailed points of emphasis and follow-up for the next session. There was no small talk.

Many times I was impressed as Dr. Steve would consult his notes and interject a vital question from a previous discussion that had occurred months ago. It was apparent he carefully reviewed his thoughts before each session. This well-trained man was the most empathic listener I have ever known. Often during our talks, he would get up while continuing the conversation, take a "random" book from his library, turn to a page and show me a passage that perfectly illustrated the issue at hand.

When I mentioned blog posts, essays, journal entries, and books I had written, he requested permission to read them, and it was evident by his questions and notes the next session that he had read every word of the text and evaluated the context. We would discuss the symbolism and layers of my current artwork that emanated from my anguish and past.

He once said that he had told *his* therapist about a particularly tricky issue we were grappling with. He explained that he regularly attended professional therapy to maintain objectivity and clarity with his clients.

When I asked his advice about an issue, he would gently and skillfully ask questions that guided me to a personal answer. He was trained that if therapy were to be effective, he must guide me to the solutions for myself.

It was apparent he was on my side. He proved it time and time again. This did not mean he would put up with my biased views, selfishness or lack of facing the truth—it merely indicated that he was a trustworthy companion during this painful journey of grief and recovery. In his most stark and honest therapeutic reflections of me—shame and judgment were conspicuously absent.

A therapist is much like a guide on the journey of life. Good guides tell us they see something ahead. Better guides give us a detailed account of what they see, but wise guides help us look for ourselves.

Four Qualities When Considering a Therapist

1) They should be encouragers.

2) They are in touch with their inner being—they question their actions and reactions, and they empathize with you.

3) They embrace good questions and guide us to the right ones.

4) They have a therapist to guide and encourage them.

Seek a therapist who is not afraid of the *right* questions. We all need someone to help us press inward—not re-press our deepest hurts, joys, and feelings. We need someone who can help us recognize and touch the hot ovens of our injuries and the chains that bind us. That is why the best therapists pause the conversation and ask the question, "What are you feeling there?" when a tear or deep emotion is touched. We do not have the courage (or many times—the objectivity or the ability) to go it alone.

People who have experienced a tragic loss of belonging and want to be healthy and find a new and better tribe should consider seeking professional help.

The first step is to carefully and methodically choose a therapist. It is vital to select one who is qualified and empathic—preferably a licensed psychologist or a psychiatrist—not a church counselor, a pastor, or life coach. A professional is best equipped with the knowledge and training to perform the psychological surgery and chemotherapy needed to treat an emotional and spiritual loss this overwhelming.

When facing a diagnostic medical procedure such as a biopsy, one carefully chooses a qualified and well-trained doctor. It is equally important to select a certified and well-educated therapist when facing a life crisis.

Effective psychotherapy needs to be provided in a way that meets a set of well-defined criteria. In a recent *American Psychological Association*[29] symposium, psychologists simplified these ingredients for the layman. I've listed them in brief and translated them into practical questions for use in evaluating mental health professionals serving you or those close to you. I've included a few of my own questions as well.

Some Questions To Ask When Getting Help

- Where did your therapist train and go to school? What degrees and licenses do they hold? Are they up to date?

- Do they have quality interpersonal skills? Effective psychotherapists are able to express themselves well. They sense what other people are thinking and feeling. They show warmth and acceptance, empathy, and a focus on the client.

- When you talk about what you're experiencing, does your therapist seem to be interested in learning how you feel?

- Can your therapist communicate with you in language that you understand?

- Does your therapist talk about you, and not themselves?

- Do you feel you can trust the therapist? We often can determine whether or not to trust someone within a few seconds of meeting them.

- What does your inner vibe tell you when you first meet this person?

- Is this someone who allows you to feel that you can have a good working relationship and that your faith in this person won't be betrayed?

- Do you sense a willingness for the therapist to establish an alliance with you?

- Though the therapist is obviously the expert, do you feel their concern about your goals in therapy and a willingness to work with you to set goals that are mutually agreed upon?

- Does your therapist take related notes in each session?

- Does the therapist inspire hope and optimism about your chances for improvement?

- Does the therapist exhibit sensitivity toward your cultural background? This includes showing respect for your experience and being aware of attitudes within your culture or community toward, for example, family relationships, religious practices, and appropriate behavior.

- Does your therapist rely on the best research evidence? Do they utilize APA's *Evidence-Based Practice Guidelines* to stay abreast of the latest developments in clinical psychology, particularly in their areas of expertise?

- Does your therapist participate in continued training and education? Most states require licensed mental health professionals to participate in continuing education to maintain their credentials.

- Does your therapist regularly attend therapy themselves?

- Ask your therapist about the specific cost and duration of the sessions.

- What is the payment and cancellation policy if you are unable to make a session?

- Ask when and how you are to remit payment.

Every therapist may not meet all of these criteria, but hopefully, with this awareness, you can better decide whether you or a loved one will receive the best possible treatment. Engaging a qualified therapist can be a crucial step for many in coping with a devastating loss of belonging. Proper counseling from a trusted advisor can provide help in finding a new and better tribe. Once again, the most critical factor in healing from loss is having the support of other people.

The Loss of Belonging: Ten Steps To A New (& Better) Tribe

II. Finding You

Step 4

In Which We Seek to Understand Being and Doing

C ontrary to popular opinion, I feel the ultimate goal of life is not doing what you love, it is becoming who you are. Our time on earth is limited. On average, we live about 27,000 days. The first 9,000 days we grow up and get an education, and the next 9,000 we work hard to establish a home, a family, and a career. Then in the blink of an eye, the last 9,000 days will suddenly be upon us.

Should you retire to play golf in Florida? Keep doing what you've been doing? Get a travel trailer? Have a mid-life crisis? Or do you dare live out your last 9,000 days being who you are and making your dreams come true? Do you attempt to ask existential questions? To search for meaning in life? To reach for your purpose?

Some of us are still in the first 9,000 days of our lives and others in the middle of the frantic busyness of the second 9,000. But do we want to spend them doing something we hate (or something we love) at the expense of being who we are?

Life is too short. It's easy to get trapped into doing the bidding of others or enslaved to the influences of the institutions of life—our family, religion, school, and society. We forget that these relationships and organizations are as fragile and unreliable as the people that support them.

Listen carefully to the words of the immortal Steve Jobs: "Don't let the noise of other opinions drown out your own inner voice. And most important, have the courage to follow your heart and intuition. They somehow already know what you truly want to become."[30]

I open my book *Ruminations* very purposefully with a quote from the great "philosopher" Jim Carrey. "Why fail at something you don't enjoy? At least fail at something you love!" It is a powerful and thought-provoking quote.

However, I would like to qualify that last sentence to say: "At least fail at *doing what you are!*"

Become Who You Are

Most of us have not been allowed to ask for answers. History has subjected us to an awful lot of know-it-alls, men (almost always men) who know what is best for everyone, who articulate what we all must think, believe, do, and avoid. As I enter my sixth decade of life, I am increasingly suspicious of those who have all the answers and will not tolerate questions.

Let's begin embracing questions, and understanding there is a difference between good questions and the right questions. Asking *good* questions can free us from the lies of societal institutions and asking the *right* questions can lead us to a life of meaning and wholeness.

A few *good* questions during my first 18,000 days were: "Do I have to stay in the isolation and poverty of the mountains in which I grew up? Must I work in the coal mines and not finish high school like everyone else? Should my job come before my family? Is all truth God's truth? Is the Bible literal? Is it true?"

As I approached mid-life, I asked, "Is this all there is to life—constant meetings and religious politics that have nothing to do with who I am?" These questions were *good* questions. They eventually led to freedom from a thirty-year career in the ministry.

Once I managed the courage to be free, however, I suddenly found that my newfound freedom became a prison. I had never been allowed to spread my wings. And I crashed. But thankfully, the suffering led to a desperation that caused me to start asking the *right* questions.

Asking the right questions can lead us to meaning. Could it be the questions and not the answers that give freedom and purpose? Good questions lead to freedom, and the right questions lead to meaning. You may ask, how can we know the right questions?

I believe the right questions are universal. They are inquiries that have been made throughout history. Men like anthropologist Donald Brown, mythologist Joseph Campbell, and psychologist James Hollis have spent their life researching these ubiquitous questions. They are questions as old as time.

These three men have identified recurring questions throughout history. Brown calls them the *Human Universals*, Campbell calls it the *Hero's Journey* and Hollis calls them the *Swamplands of the Soul*. It's why I spent hundreds of hours creating a resource, *God I Have A Question...or Two* to help identify universal questions to ask yourself, others, and your god(s).

If we can manage the courage (and endure the suffering) to begin this quest for meaning, we will find the goal of life is not happiness or success or even doing what you love. The purpose of life is meaning. It's ironic that many of these questions come out only later in life after intense suffering and expensive psychotherapy.

It takes wise and experienced guides to help us break the chains of institutional lies. The lies we've been told as truth by those we trust can be dangerous and volatile. Mainly when spoken by those we have been taught to give unquestioning respect: our teachers, our preachers, our culture, and yes, even our family.

Most of these influencers don't intend to lie to us, but they do. Indeed, they've been lied to as well. We underestimate the power of the institutions of our lives to restrict us. They confine us to the past, contaminate the present, and consume our future. We must break the shackles of the past.

When well-meaning people tell us to "cut the apron strings" we know all too well, these are not mere strings—they are an endless tangle of rusty chains. We are prisoners of our history.

Who can forget the first view of the pod in the iconic movie *The Matrix*? I will always remember the chill that settled over me as I saw those thousands and thousands of adults imprisoned in pods, covered in embryonic fluid, and attached to the umbilical cords of masters they never wanted.

Four Chains We Need To Break

1. The Chains of Family

Pat Conroy published *The Great Santini* in 1976, and it later became a film starring Robert Duvall. Conroy featured his father in the novel-memoir and gave the rest of his family supporting roles.

According to Pat, his father—whom he'd immortalized as the tyrannical Colonel "Bull" Meecham —called him after reading each chapter to ask in a choked voice why he hated him so much. Pat's mother, Peg, was horrified and stopped speaking to him altogether.

In person, it is said that Pat Conroy is like your best pal. But he somehow found the guts to write candidly about himself and his family. His tribe shunned him, and his Mom's devoutly Christian relatives handed out pamphlets at his book signings urging customers not to buy his book. They wanted nothing more to do with him.

Conroy's Mom divorced her husband of thirty-three years in the aftermath, and Pat himself went into therapy soon after the book appeared. On balance, he said the whole Conroy clan reacted to his novel about them by having "a collective nervous breakdown."[31] But *The Great Santini* has become one of the most influential books in modern history, and it gave Pat Conroy the opportunity to break the confining chain of his familial past.

2. The Chains of Religion

A few years ago I was asked by *EMI Record*s to do a television interview of a young lady named Vicky Beeching. Ironically, that interview has the distinction of being my most-viewed *YouTube* video. Vicky was a relatively unknown recording artist and songwriter who had recently signed her first record deal with *Worship Together—EMI's* Christian imprint.

I was impressed not only by her extraordinary physical beauty, but also by her engaging charisma, gentleness, and kindness. An Oxford graduate with a degree in theology, she possessed that all too rare chemistry that comes from a vast intellect, a deep humility, and a delightful English accent inflected with the muse of Chaucer's Canterbury.

We later became good friends, and she asked me to mentor her in social media. As her career progressed, her layered and beautiful songwriting earned the majority of her income. In 2009 she was diagnosed with morphea, an autoimmune disease brought on by internal stress and returned to the UK to receive eighteen months of chemotherapy. The treatment was successful, but the life-threatening illness forced her to evaluate her life.

By a series of events she was hired by the BBC and is now a sought-after commentator on issues related to ethics, technology, women, Christianity, music, and social media. She is also finishing a PhD with a dual emphasis in Christianity and sexuality.

In August 2014, this theologian who spends holy days with the Archbishop of Canterbury, and whose God-fearing lyrics are sung by millions in America's Bible Belt, came out as a lesbian. And she has been crucified.

Boycotts of her music were already in place since Vicky decided to speak up for same-sex marriage during the previous year, and they have taken away much of her ongoing income. Hatred has been flung at her online by religious people: "You are possessed by the devil," is a typical comment. I watched with horror a chilling, shame-spewing video by a "religious leader" about her coming out.

But in Vicky's words, "What Jesus taught was a radical message of welcome and inclusion and love. I feel certain God loves me just the way I am. When I think of myself at age sixteen, sobbing into that carpet, as the church tried to exorcize my attraction towards women, I just want to help anyone in that situation to not have to go through what I did, to show that instead, you can be yourself—a person of integrity."[32] Her courageous story is now a best-selling book, *Undivided: Coming Out, Becoming Whole, and Living Free from Shame.*[33]

In my own memoir, *A Renaissance Redneck In A Mega-Church Pulpit*, I write "religious ideas are curious things. They flow in ruts worn deep by time and habit, and the rare men (and women) who have the character to propose to divert them by reason and argument have a long contract on their hands."

Religion, as Vicky and I know it, is a way of life where *no* is said with such constancy that on some days, one might forget the affirmative is even a possibility. The question of restrictions, of what is allowed and not allowed, is very much at the heart of the story of religion. It is a parable about the nature of control.

To become who we truly are, we must break the confining chains of our religious past.

3. The Chains of Education

Sir Ken Robinson, in his challenging *Ted* talk, *Do Schools Kill Creativity?*[34] says: "We have a system of education modeled on the industrial age. Schools are still pretty much organized on factory lines—ringing bells, separate facilities, specialized into separate subjects and the idea of one answer. We still educate children by batches. We need to give our children the ability to see lots of possible answers to a question, to think divergently, to think not just in linear ways, to see multiple solutions, not one."

Walt Disney hated high school so much that he sent a letter to his principal telling him how "disgusted" he was by it.[35] Starting to dabble in the entertainment industry by age fourteen, Walt and his friend Russell put a down-payment on a movie camera and intended to begin making children's films.

Frustrated with school, Walt decided to set his course, and pursue work as an artist, in particular as a newspaper cartoonist. His father was horrified at the impracticality of this plan. He fully intended for Walt to work at his jelly company.

But in Walt's words, "I was able to...line right up on an objective...and I went for it." By age seventeen Disney had his dream and was ready to make it come true. The rest, as they say—is history. Walt Disney's dream did come true far beyond even *his* wildest imaginings. By having the courage to *be who he was,* he has helped all of us wish upon a star.

There is no one path in life. Healthy tribes depend upon people with a variety of talents. Ironically, the personality tests developed during the Industrial Age to weed out people who would not conform to the assembly line, have now provided a means to determine your uniquenesses and to help think divergently. When you follow your own true course, you create new opportunities, meet different people, have different experiences, and are better equipped to find a new and better tribe.

4. The Chains of Society

Consider the immortal words of Nelson Mandela, a man who grew up and defied the racist society of South Africa: "I have fought against white domination, and I have fought against black domination. I have cherished the ideal of a democratic and free society in which all persons live together in harmony and with equal opportunities. It is an ideal which I hope to live for and to achieve. But if need be, it is an ideal for which I am prepared to die."[36]

To live life is to make decisions, yet who really makes most of our choices? Everyone makes their own, is the obvious response. However, this is not exactly right. For better or worse, society affects the decisions we make and the ideals we cherish—from what we buy, to the careers we choose, to what we eat, to what we fight for.

In *Invisible Influence: The Hidden Forces that Shape Behavior*[37], Jonah Berger, a marketing professor at the *Wharton School of Business* traces the myriad ways that social forces guide us, often without our knowledge.

Berger says, "If you're like most people, you think that your choices and behaviors are driven by your personal tastes and opinions. You wear a certain jacket because you liked the way it looked. You picked a particular career because you found it interesting. The notion that our choices are driven by our own personal thoughts and opinions is patently obvious. Right? Wrong."

"Without our realizing it, other people's behavior has a huge influence on everything we do at every moment of our lives, from the mundane to the momentous occasion. Even strangers have a startling impact on our judgments and decisions: our attitudes toward a welfare policy shift if we're told it is supported by Democrats versus Republicans (even though the policy is the same in both cases)."[38]

Berger integrates research and thinking from business, psychology, and social science to focus on the subtle, invisible influences behind our choices as individuals. By understanding how social influence works, we can decide when to resist and when to embrace it—and how we can use this knowledge to make better-informed decisions and exercise more control over our own behavior.

It is possible to break the chains of society and become who we are.

No Regrets

We previously read the words of Steve Jobs as he said to have the courage to follow our heart and intuition—but we are afraid. We're worried we will look ridiculous. We're scared to try. We are terrified we may fail. Breaking the chains of family, religion, education, and society while finding your passion takes courage. But what if the only fearlessness you need is the audacity to be who you are? Wouldn't you do everything possible to live an unfettered life?

After way too many years of unfulfilling work, Bronnie Ware began searching for a job with meaning. Despite having no formal qualifications or experience, she found herself working in *Hospice* care. The years spent tending to the needs of those who were dying transformed Bronnie's life.

In her book, *The Top Five Regrets of the Dying* she expresses how significant these regrets are and how we can address these issues while we still have time. Ware writes of the extraordinary clarity of vision that people gain at the end of their lives, and how we might learn from their wisdom.

"When questioned about any regrets they had or anything they would do differently," she says, "common themes surfaced again and again." According to Ware, here is the top regret of the dying: *I wish I'd had the courage to live a life true to myself, not the life others expected of me.*

She writes, "This was the most common regret of all. When people realize that their life is almost over and look back clearly on it, they see how many dreams went unfulfilled. Most people had not honored even half their dreams and had to die knowing that it was due to choices they had made—or not made. Health and success bring a numbing to our life that we don't realize until we no longer have it."[39]

A Personal Journey

Soon after the horror of *9/11*, at the age of forty-three (mid-life), I embarked on a trip to a Muslim country in Central Asia called Kyrgyzstan. I had never heard of it, I did not feel comfortable flying, and I'm a homebody. But for some reason, I went.

As our group cleared security at Heathrow in London for the second leg of our journey, there a delay because even the seasoned British guard had never seen the FRU airport code for Bishkek, the capital city of Kyrgyzstan. Let's say it is not a well-known mecca of tourism.

After twenty-eight hours of grueling travel, the last eighteen as the only Westerners in a plane crammed full of burkha-garbed Easterners and exotic body odors—we stepped off the plane into a desolate land, only to wearily hop into an old van with balding tires for another harrowing eight-hour drive into towering mountains along a road filled with potholes and steep bluffs with no guard rails.

We finally arrived at Karakol, a village nestled in the mighty Tian Shan Mountain Range. I was literally in the middle of nowhere. If you place a finger on a globe on the opposite side of the world from Nashville, it would be right around Kyrgyzstan.

It was amid this profound fatigue and fear of an alien Muslim world that I experienced a moment of enlightenment. My assignment during the trip was to present a lecture to college students at a Muslim University about the arts and free enterprise.

It was easy to see that all of the art in this third-world country was utilitarian. There were crude pictures of their homes called yurts, simple paintings of rugs with the Kyrgyz symbol, and undeveloped sketches of the mountains. There was no concept of creating art for art's sake.

For the first time in the contemporary history of their country, these students had the freedom to be artists. As my words channeled through a Kyrgyz interpreter, you could have heard a pin drop.

The "college" classroom was far more primitive than the one-room schoolhouses of my Appalachian heritage. The desks were too small for the students, and the concrete floor was frigid. Looking out the smoky and broken panes of glass, I could see rivers of human excrement running down the streets.

There are still moments when I catch a similar smell, and it instantly transports me back to that moment. I had never witnessed poverty at this level, even in the Appalachians. Hopelessness filled the eyes of older people, and most of them were bleary from the effects of cheap Russian vodka.

But the students huddled in this dingy classroom had a glimmer of hope in their eyes. As I talked about the beauty and uniqueness of their flora and fauna and the architectural grandeur of the multi-colored Russian Orthodox cathedral in the center of their town, their faces filled with pride and hope.

I had landed in a country the world had forgotten, and if that wasn't enough, I had driven eight hours farther into the middle of nothingness, surrounded by a seemingly impenetrable mountain range. I was shivering from the frigid cold—snowflakes flying—while walking through streets paved with mud.

The drab and depressing grays of disintegrating communist-era buildings lined the mucky streets. But I was tingling with life. I felt alive! I was scared, alone, and conspicuously American in a village that is now off-limits because of the strong *Al-Queda* presence, but I was alive.

Why?

I had somehow inspired people in the middle of despair. If my words could encourage the youth in this bleak town, I knew they could work anywhere on earth. I didn't want to go back home to endless meetings that had nothing to do with me, to pointless arguments and petty politics. I had found my reason for being—the life I needed to live. The job I was doing was not who I was. Soon after returning to America, I began preparations to walk away from my lucrative but unfulfilling career as Pastor of Creative Arts in one of America's largest mega-churches.

I'm here as living proof that you can be who you are and not what you do. You can feel something, you can burst through the anesthesia, and prove to yourself that you are not asleep. We can stand on the shoulders of giants such as Steve Jobs, Pat Conroy, Vicky Beeching, Walt Disney, Nelson Mandela, and Bronnie Ware. What questions do you need to ask? What chains do you need to break?

Listen to the words of Walt Disney, "The more you like yourself, the less you are like anyone else, which makes you unique. All the adversity I've had in my life, all my troubles and obstacles, have strengthened me. You may not realize it when it happens, but a kick in the teeth may be the best thing in the world for you. We did Disneyland, in the knowledge that most of the people I talked to thought it would be a financial disaster—closed and forgotten within the first year, but you reach a point where you don't work for money."[40]

Your dreams can come true if you dare to pursue them. This crucial step to finding a new and better tribe is about having the courage to accept who you are and what your dreams are—not what others think they should be. Have the courage to live a life true to yourself, not the life others expect of you. Be who you are.

Step 5

In Which We Seek To Understand A Sense of Self

Digital companies such as *Google* and *Facebook* make millions of dollars providing companies with extensive profiles of their clients. These tech companies know us better than we know ourselves. Assuming you feed them an average amount of information, they know your age, gender, where you live, your social circle, what you do for a living, and your general interests.

Thanks to the popularity of *Google Maps*, the company has a detailed account of every place you've been. *Google* dominance in search, video (*YouTube*), email (*Gmail*), and entrance into television (*YouTubeTV*) provides rich data for them to play with. The companies have a substantial record of any event you've attended in the past thanks to *Google Calendar* and *Facebook Events*.

It may come as a surprise to know that both companies offer the option to download a file with (almost) everything they know about you.[41] When I downloaded and compared the two, my *Google* profile came in at a staggering 17.5GB, *or roughly the size of nine million Word documents*, while my Facebook profile was 600MB which equates to about 400,000 *Word* documents.

These strangers have hundreds of thousands of documents about us. But I wonder, how many do we have about ourselves? Only the most diligent of us routinely record facts and feelings about our self in a physical or digital journal. Most of humanity has little or no personal reflection of their existence.

In seeking to understand a sense of self (self-perception), we must ask these questions. What's going on in my body, mind, spirit, and soul? What's my physical, mental, spiritual, and emotional life like? What do I think about life in general; my own experience in particular? What meaning or purpose do I find? Am I happy and fulfilled, or am I discontented? What are the values and dreams that form my attitude about existence? What are my loves, my hates? Have I any idea *who* I am as an individual? Do I know how to become my own person?

Why are these invaluable questions difficult for most of us to ask? Why have we not taken the time to ask them?

First, the institutions of life have taught us to frown on self-evaluation. As I previously mentioned, it is interesting to note that the personality tests we now utilize for personal growth were first developed for use in industry to screen out applicants who would create workplace disturbances.[42] The companies felt that excessive self-awareness led to emotional maladjustment.

We have not been encouraged by the institutions of western culture to understand a sense of self. Religion demands self-denial, education promotes cloning, the family teaches dependency, and society fosters conformity.

Second, researching the essentials that comprise the self requires a commitment of time that most people don't have or will not take; the world would soon grind to a halt if we all embarked upon a lifelong search to find our selves.

Third, to come to know our self requires seasons of intense self-scrutiny. It is impossible to discern what makes us 'tick' without recognizing the essence of our physical and mental responses to life and understanding the highly personal inner aspects of spiritual values and emotional reactions.

Full awareness of the external and internal sensations, actions, and surroundings that give us meaning is psychologically deep and multi-layered. Professor Graham Collier says, "The search for the essential self requires a 'Sherlock Holmes' mentality and discipline: it's a hell of a job to unify outer and inner 'consciousnesses.'"[43] However, most of us can better know who we are (gain a sense of self) if we have a few fundamental principles of understanding.

- First, we must understand the restricting power of institutions such as religion, society, family, and education.
- Second, we must make a commitment to allocate time for an internal quest.
- Third, we must regularly practice self-evaluation.

Perhaps it's time to clarify some terms. The words ego and self are easily confused and can be challenging to understand. Few people have influenced contemporary psychology like Carl Jung. The favorite staple of personality tests today, the *Myers-Briggs Type Indicator* (MBTI) derived from his body of work.[44]

Carl Jung and Sigmund Freud had radically different ideas about these two psychological terms. In Jungian theory, which will serve as the basis of thought in this book, the ego is only one aspect of the self. Freud however, believed the ego performed all the functions of the self.

According to Jung, the ego represents the conscious mind. The ego, I refer to it in this book as our *center*, is like a "central command station," organizing our thoughts, feelings, senses, and intuition.[45]

However, it is important to reiterate that the *ego is only one small portion of the self.* Jung believed that the ego is the part of the self that selects the most relevant information from the environment and chooses a direction to take based on the knowledge. He agreed with Freud that a person's past and childhood experiences determine behavior, but he also believed that we are shaped by our future aspirations.[46]

For Jung, the ultimate aim of every individual is to achieve a state of selfhood (a sense of self). Jungian expert James Hollis writes, "Jung called it *individuation,* that is, the lifelong project of becoming more nearly the whole person we were meant to be—what the gods intended, not our parents or our tribe. Our individuation summons each of us to stand in the presence of our own mystery, and become more fully responsible for who we are in this journey we call our life."[47]

He says, "If we are prepared to take on the daunting task of the personal journey of liberation and individuation, we will be able to move beyond our personal history and manifest our full potential. The goal of individuation is **wholeness**, not an ego that reigns and keeps the psyche fragmented."[48] We will talk more about fragmentation and wholeness in Step 6.

Once again, the basic principles to becoming who we are: we must gain the courage to break the stranglehold of the institutions of life, allocate time in our busy schedule to explore the mystery of our self, and if need be, find a qualified therapist to assist us in this quest.

A qualified therapist can help discover a sense of self and determine what brings meaning to life—but you must specifically request assistance. I asked my psychologist, Dr. Steve, to guide me to the essentials that best describe my purpose in life. Self-evaluation and distilling one's essence to a few words, symbols, or phrases requires thoughtful and at times stressful work.

Jung's writings and journals introduced me to an invaluable tool which we explore in the next chapter—an ancient and time-honored roadmap to wholeness. It was this simple instrument that helped me grasp the essential aspects of my being: freedom, curiosity, communion, and sensuality.

I hope this Jungian introduction will serve as a catalyst for your "daunting task of a personal journey," and serve as an encouragement to embark upon the initial stages of a long but rewarding path to wholeness and a sense of self.

Let's go back a moment to the concept Jesus Christ expresses in the great commandment: The prerequisite for loving others is loving yourself. I would further posit, the precondition to *knowing* others is a knowledge of your self. The logical progression is first to find ourselves, and only then can we effectively continue the journey to find a new (and better) tribe.

It is important to note that a loss of belonging can be the motivation for a renewed sense of self. Ironically, it was my personal individuation process that ultimately led to a divorce and the loss of my tribe. This odyssey is not for the faint of heart.

To articulate a sense of self requires knowing the words that describe your ego (your center), your essentials, and your layers. Let's begin with your ego—your center.

1. What is *the* word that describes your ego— your center?

In addition to an empathic and caring therapist, there are several ways to discover your center.

- Have your closest and most trustworthy confidants describe you using only **one** word. Write each word down. Look for recurring and similar terms.

- Journal every moment that brings a verklempt (this Yiddish word means to be overwhelmed by emotion, perhaps so much that one cannot speak), a tear to your eye, or a catch in your throat. It could be something like a beautiful sunset, a scene in a movie, a commercial, or an affirmation. When you have journaled a significant number, look for a pattern. This pattern will provide clues to your center.

- Utilize multiple personality assessments such as the *Enneagram, DISC, Meyers-Briggs, StrengthFinder, and Shape*. While no one personality assessment (that divides the entire human race into a few categories) can fully capture the nuances of a unique person, when used in combination they can provide clues to your center by revealing commonalities that recur in every assessment.

- List professions or careers you would choose if the sky was the limit. Then ask why?

- If you dared to live a life true to yourself, and not the life others expected of you, what would it look like? Take some time to strip away the chains of the institutions of life that have censored, repressed, and imprisoned you. Journal your thoughts.

- What are you hungry for? What is your strongest desire? Be honest (with no disclaimers) and use words to describe this soulish question.

- Now look for common words from all these exercises that intuitively and rationally feel right. Distill them down. Then again ask trustworthy confidants which word they think best describes who you are at your center.

We will use this word as we fashion a visual representation of the self. Don't worry if you are not yet sure about the exact word. As we progress, it could change. But do your best to identify the word that seems to describe your *center* at this time.

Write the word here:

_____

Write the word in a digital notebook or utilizing the note feature if reading the Kindle version. It is important to write it down and then say out loud,

"I am _____.

2. What are the words that describe your self —your essentials?

Various ideologies number the parts of a human being as two, three, or four. For example, some theologians refer to a three-part outline based on the Holy Trinity (Spirit, Soul, and Body). Jesus Christ in his teaching in Mark 12:30 seems to delineate four parts: Strength (Body), Mind, Heart (Spirit), and Soul.

But modern scientists increasingly dispute the existence of an eternal soul. Professor and author Yuval Noah Harari suggests in his mind-bending book *Homo Deus*[49] that we are: Body, Algorithm, and Mind. Others insist there are only two parts of the self: Body and Mind.

A few historical examples of the essentials of the self are the Three Hares of the fifth century that possibly originated in China. There are Three (but sometimes Four) Monkeys, said to derive from an ancient Japanese culture that predates Christ. The numbers two, three, and four recur throughout history, archaeology, theology, philosophy, and in the scientific and physical world. These dyads, triads, and tetrads have permeated culture from the beginning of civilization.

Whatever the number you accept, it makes sense to utilize words and concepts to describe and symbolize your essence, your self. I call those descriptive words our *essentials*. Perhaps it's my musical background, my religious upbringing, or only a matter of choice, but for the purpose of this book, I will utilize a tetrad (a set of four): Body, Mind, Spirit, and Soul.

Feel free to utilize dyads, triads, tetrads, or any other number of words that best fits your belief and provides inner clarity as you continue this journey. We will begin a discovery of these words, that best express your essentials in Step 6.

3. What are the words that symbolize the layers of your being?

Human nature is composed of tetrads. A tetrad is a fancy word for a group of four. These tetrads naturally occur throughout the wallpaper of our universe. In botany (meiosis), chemistry (tetravalent atom), music (four parts of harmony), art (four primary colors), biology (four blood types), nature (four seasons), and the natural world (four elements).

I believe the tetrads (the essentials) in human life are: physical, mental, emotional and spiritual. We need to understand all four of these essentials within ourselves better to regain wholeness and belonging in our lives.

Some common tetrads (sets of four) that can provide symbols of understanding for the layers of our self include:

- The Four Seasons: Winter, Spring, Summer, and Fall
- The Four Elements: Earth, Wind, Fire, and Water
- The Four Cardinal Directions: North, South, East, and West
- The Primary Psychological Colors: Red, Green, Blue, and Yellow
- A Sense of Place: Geographical, Demographical, Psychological, and Ideological
- The Four Parts of Musical Harmony: Soprano, Alto, Tenor, and Bass
- The Primary Food Groups: Milk, Meat, Fruits, and Bread
- The Four Major Mathematical Operations: Addition, Subtraction, Multiplication, and Division
- The Four Cardinal Virtues: Justice, Prudence, Fortitude and Temperance
- The Four Fundamental Personality Types: Sanguine, Choleric, Melancholic, and Phlegmatic

Again, we will begin a discovery of these words, your layers in Step 6. For many of us reading this book, our journey takes place amid a complicated past, the distractions of a frenzied society, and the heartbreaking experience of the loss of belonging.

But remember, it is crucial to allocate time in our lives to ask these questions if we want to find a new and better tribe. What's going on in my body, mind, spirit, and soul? What's my physical, mental, spiritual, and emotional life like? What do I think about life in general; my own experience in particular? What meaning or purpose do I find? Am I happy and fulfilled, or am I discontented? What are the values and dreams that form my attitude about existence? What are my loves, my hates? Have I any idea *who* I am as an individual? Do I know how to become my own person?

The intent of this book—finding a new and (better) tribe—points out that a prerequisite to belonging is a conscious and more mindful relationship to your sense of self (you), and *then* a sense of place (others.) The terms and questions we have discovered in this step will guide us to Step 6.

Step 6

In Which We Seek To Identify Our Essentials

I n steps 6 and 7, we will identify the essential layers of our self by utilizing an ancient and time-honored symbol. We will use common tetrads (groups of four) to begin a journey to find our self. You may want to add more layers later to reflect the extraordinary nuances of who you are.

First, let's talk about fragmentation and wholeness. We are a divided world full of fragmented people. Our brokenness and complacency have unwittingly enabled our politicians and media to create divisive mosaics using pairs of opposite colors and phrases. Red or blue states, blue or white collar, white or black skin, educated or uneducated, man or woman, Christian or Muslim, Republican or Democrat, weak or strong, rich or poor, liberal or conservative, socialist or progressive, pro-life or pro-choice, gay or straight, to name only a few.

> *"Where there is no desire or pursuit, there is no wholeness, but there are satisfactory lesser states, fragments."*
>
> —Gore Vidal.[50]

We cannot be satisfied with lesser states, with a fragmented life. Our forefathers have worked in vain for wholeness in politics, careers, race, education, gender, religion, factions, strength, materialism, ideologies, and sexual identity. Today, most of us feel more fragmented and more cynical than ever before.

However, there is hope. In color theory, opposite colors are called complementary colors. In the world of color, contradictions make beautiful and inspirational statements. We have all heard the term "opposites attract." You can't have the yin without the yang. They balance each other through warm and cool characteristics that are often simultaneously stimulating and pleasing to the eye. The contrast can be bold and energetic, or it can be soft and soothing.[51]

I remain hopeful that our world teeters on the precipice of a new beginning, that is, a fundamental change of attitude toward the values and meaning of life. After years of thinking others have all the answers, we are desperately beginning to look within ourselves.

Physicist Stephen Hawking says, "When we see the world from space, we see ourselves as a whole. We see unity and not divisions. It is such a simple image with a compelling message; one planet, one human race."[52]

These external divisions seep into our internal self-perception. This could be the most urgent question we face in the twenty-first century: How, in all this fragmentation, all this division, can we lead lives of wholeness? Wholeness as it pertains to all aspects of our self, especially our physical, intellectual, spiritual, and emotional development.

We need to ask the *right* questions.

- What would a life of wholeness look like?
- How do we understand wholeness?
- How do we begin the path to put our lives back together?
- What could you do to make your life more meaningful and more cohesive?

What if I told you there is a simple yet profound device for looking inward and that people in Eastern cultures have been using it with great success for thousands of years.

I heard the term *mandala* (pronounced **muhn**-du-luh) mentioned sporadically throughout my life, but I never took the time to understand it. My fuzzy view was some sort of irrelevant New Age mumbo-jumbo. It didn't seem my kind of thing. But then three years ago a *House of Cards* television episode portrayed Tibetan monks creating an exquisite sand design as part of an exchange visit.

Every time Frank or Claire Underwood passed by them in the White House, they were fascinated by the aura of tranquility as this art came to life. The monks' creation was called a sand mandala, and its primary function is healing and purification.

The *Bustle* website explains: "This particular mandala is unique to Tibetan Buddhism. Monks first create a drawing and then fill it in with colorful sand. But this isn't like your summer camp sand art. Grains of sand are carefully placed along the picture with funnels, tubes, and scrapers over several days.

Once it's completed, the mandala is blessed, and the sand is swept away and disposed of in water in what's called a *Dissolution Ceremony*. Yup, all that work is just destroyed like a sand castle at the beach. But it's all part of the healing process."[53]

The ritual of destroying a mandala symbolizes the impermanence of existence or in the context of this book, the impermanence of belonging. It brings to mind the words to one of my favorite songs:

I close my eyes, only for a moment,
and the moment's gone
All my dreams pass before my eyes,
a curiosity
Dust in the wind
All they are is dust in the wind
Same old song, just a drop of water
in an endless sea
All we do crumbles to the ground
though we refuse to see
Dust in the wind
All we are is dust in the wind
Now, don't hang on, nothing lasts forever
but the earth and sky
It slips away
And all your money won't another minute buy
Dust in the wind
All we are is dust in the wind
All we are is dust in the wind
Dust in the wind
Everything is dust in the wind
Everything is dust in the wind.[54]

At the request of the Dalai Lama, twenty Buddhist monks from the Drepung Loseling Monastery constructed a sand mandala at the Smithsonian Museum in response to the September 11 tragedies. This seven-foot-square mandala, one of the largest ever created in the West, was offered for the healing and protection of America.

In the book *Carl Jung: A Very Short Introduction* by Anthony Stevens, I found that the eminent psychologist utilized the symbol of the mandala as a path to individuation, to a sense of self. Remember, individuation is the lifelong project of becoming more nearly the whole person we were meant to be—what the gods intended, not the parents or the tribe.

Jung began to understand the mandala as a representation of the inner Self, the central nucleus of the personality. He went so far as to build a home in Bolligen, Switzerland which after many additions over the years became an architectural mandala. A central tower housed his private library and office, and the addition of wings eventually formed the symbol as a whole.

Mandalas have been found all over the world and utilized in different faiths. *CarlJung.net* says, "We see it in Christianity using frescos with animal images representing apostles. The astrologic zodiac and its versions are examples of a mandala. In the Indian spiritual practices, we find fascinating examples of the mandala, with symbols of the local pantheon. In yoga practices, a mandala can be a support for meditation or an image that must be internalized through mental absorption. This image organizes the inner energies and forces of the practitioner and puts them in a relationship with their ego-consciousness."[55]

The website *Mandalas for the Soul* tells us, "The circle shape of the mandala has been used in cultures around the world as a form of spiritual practice. While some of the most common examples come from Asia, there is also a rich history of the use of mandalas in Native American culture. The Aztec cultures of Central and South America used the shape of the mandala to create their grand calendars and to record religious principles. Many tribes throughout the Northern American landscape also used mandalas as ways to connect with the gods."[56]

"The original Native American medicine wheels/mandalas were stone artifacts built by the aboriginal peoples who lived in what is now the northwestern United States and southwestern Canada. They were first called "medicine wheels" in the 1800s. In Native American usage, medicine means anything that promotes harmony, and illness is seen as disharmony within a person or between a person and his or her relations. Medicine wheels took several forms, but most had a central stone cairn, one or more concentric stone circles, and several stone lines radiating outward from the center. The Ellis medicine wheel, built by the aboriginal Blackfoot Indians, was radiocarbon dated to about 1400 A. D."[57]

For those with a Christian worldview, "the symbolism of the cross needs little amplification: it indicates the cardinal points of the mandala and is the Christian symbol of wholeness, representing the reconciliation of opposites through suffering, the memorial of Christ's individuation and atonement with God. The cross stands for the path of submission to one's personal destiny as a human being."[58]

The idea to use the mandala regularly as a way to evaluate and find my self prompted me to purchase Jung's *Red Book*,[59] a massive tome that contains every mandala Jung created. As I perused this book, I drew my first mandala to represent my sense of self—it included a rough sketch of my center, my essentials, and my layers. After a few iterations, the value of this helpful tool began to materialize before my eyes.

Many jobs come with feedback mechanisms built-in: a quarterly performance review, a software-generated weekly numbers report, or a group presentation session. It makes sense to create a regular evaluation of our self. We are always growing and changing. Conducting a personal feedback analysis is a straightforward activity for understanding a sense of self and improving self-awareness.

In using the mandala as a guide to wholeness, it is helpful to think of it as a mirror. We can view the wheel as a reflection of our whole self—the essence of who we are. The symbolism and goal of the circle is interrelated harmony between the core and the essentials of the self. The four quadrants of the circle can represent the cohesive essentials of our self and can be nuanced with layers such as elements, directions, colors, seasons, and more.

If this seems a bit complicated, don't worry, it will become more evident as we create our own mandalas in the next section. I believe everyone can begin the path to wholeness by understanding the layers of our lives with this invaluable tool. It is a graphical representation of the Self (as Carl Jung calls our inner being). It can appear in dreams and visions, or it can be spontaneously created as a work of art.[60]

A mandala in our context is a symbol of the self in its ideal form. Its creation guides the transformation of a fragmented being into one of wholeness. This graphical representation can be used as a pathway or a roadmap, helping us envision and know a sense of self. Generally speaking, a mandala is a geometrical form—a circle. Much like viewing our world from outer space, it is a simple image with a compelling message. It is a circle of life, and most symbols of self are based on a cycle of death and rebirth.

In modern times a mandala can be compared to a sophisticated GPS for our self—a symbol that inspires something within us, a sacred map to help us recognize our self and our place in this world. The mandala provides the path that can help us return to the ancient and fundamental inner relationship from which we have strayed.

Especially in these divided times, harmony must be restored. During such times, mandalas can guide you to listen to your inner voice and find yourself. Once you better understand your self, you are on the road to finding a new and better tribe. In the next step, you will learn how to create a mandala as an evaluation of the self and to guide your path to wholeness.

The Importance of Symbols

Before we begin our essentials, let's talk about symbols. "Symbols are marks, signs or words that indicate, signify, or represent an idea, object, or relationship. Symbols allow us to go beyond what is known or seen by creating interrelationships between otherwise different concepts and experiences. A computer icon is a graphic symbol on a computer display screen that represents an app, an object (such as a file), or a function (such as the command to save)."[61]

In cultural life, an eagle is the symbol of power, a dove is the symbol of peace, a lion is the symbol of fear and strength. The American flag's white stripes symbolize the thirteen colonies of America and the stars symbolize the fifty states. In our daily life, we use colors as symbols: red is the symbol of fear and passion. Black is the color that symbolizes evil and death. Purple denotes royalty and white stands for purity.

We use flowers as symbols. For example, red roses are the ultimate expression of abiding love, and fresh white flowers are most closely associated with purity. The delicate white blossoms represent honesty, purity, and perfection.[62]

Violets symbolize modesty. The purple flower represents spiritual wisdom, faithfulness, and humility which are meanings that can be seen depicted in religious works of art. Lilies symbolize humility and devotion, and as the flowers most often associated with funerals, lilies symbolize that the soul of the departed has received restored innocence after death.[63]

Symbols can help us visualize a more complete picture of who we are. They flesh out the nuances of our life. Adding layers to our essentials provide what I call "glimpses of Eureka," offering unexpected insights and revelations during the journey to our sense of self.

It can be enlightening to consider which symbols are part of your life, which ones affect you, or which phrases you are drawn to. Take particular notice of common metaphors utilized in your speech. Are you always saying "I'm an old soul," or "I'm a free spirit"? Ask yourself why you utilize those comparisons? Try doing some journaling and see what comes up.

1. Understanding the Essentials

As I entered mid-life and the "obligatory" crisis that comes with it, I journaled that I felt like a piece of paper torn into little scraps and thrown into the wind. The fragments of my life were chaotic. About the time I was finally able to think coherently, a friend gave me a book called *Essentialism*. In it, author Greg McKeown writes these three words: "Less but better."

He goes on to say, "Essentialism is not about how to get more things done, it's about how to the get the right things done. It doesn't mean just doing less for the sake of less either. It is about making the wisest possible investment of your time and energy to operate at our highest point of contribution by doing only what is essential."[64]

Let's make the wisest possible investment of our time and energy and explore the essentials of our being.

Our **physical essential** is the body. It includes our ability to survive in the material world. Developing the physical level of our being involves learning to take good care of our bodies and enjoy them. It means developing the skills to live comfortably and effectively in the world.

 Our **mental essential** is the mind, our ability to think and reason. Developing the mental level of our being allows us to think clearly, ask questions, remain open-minded, and discern intelligently.

Our **spiritual essential** is the spirit, the part of us that exists beyond time and space. It connects us with the universal source and the oneness of all life. Our spirit is about ethical living according to personal moral guidelines. Our values and beliefs may be sacred or secular. For some, this comes in the form of religious or spiritual teachings, and for others, it is a secular ethic of responsibility.

Developing awareness of the spiritual level of our being allows us to experience a feeling of "belonging" in the universe, to acknowledge a deeper meaning and purpose in our lives.[65]

Our **emotional essential** is the soul. The ability to experience life deeply, to relate to our self, one another and the world on a feeling level. Developing the emotional level of our being allows us to appreciate the full range of the human experience with the five senses.

All four of these essentials are of equal importance. If we desire to feel whole, find meaning in life, and regain belonging, we need to focus time and attention on understanding, identifying, healing and integrating each aspect of our self.

Some layers may need extra attention because we are wounded or have suffered trauma in that area. For example, strict religious beliefs may have injured you, and as a result, you reject the spiritual aspect of life. All of us have suffered disappointment or hurt that has left us emotionally injured and fragmented.

Take a few moments to consider which of your four essentials are well-developed and which one(s) might need a little more attention or expression in your life. It is helpful to know that your essentials will be in flux as you grow and change during individuation—your growth process.

2. Identifying the Essentials

Body: Are you physically healthy and active? Do you like your body? Do you feel comfortable in your skin? Do you enjoy your sexuality? Are you able to rest peacefully? Are you a foodie? Do you have physical phobias? Allergies? Are you in good shape? Are you well-coiffed?

List eight words that best describe your body—your physical self. Immediately following the eight blank lines are some concepts to help jumpstart your thinking.

1._____   5._____

2._____   6._____

3._____   7._____

4._____   8._____

Agile
Animated
Athletic
Aristocratic bearing
Attractive
Balance
Body scent (pheromones)
Casual
Competitive
Confident (head high up)
Demonstrative
Endurance (stamina)
Energetic
Exercise
Expressive

Fitness
Flexibility
Frenetic
Graceful (motion)
Health
Height
Hygiene
Hyperactive
Image-conscious
Mobility
Neat
Posture
Powerful
Radiant
Sensual

Sexy	Style
Slow-moving	Symmetry
Smile	Verbal
Speed	Voice
Strength	Youthful

Next, narrow it down to the top four words that best describe your body—your physical self.

1._____

2._____

3._____

4._____

Now choose the ONE word that epitomizes your body—your physical self.

1._____

Mind: Are you satisfied with your intellect? Can you think and express yourself clearly? Do you have a knowledge system that supports you and works for you? Are you open to new ideas? Are you a questioner?

List eight words that best describe your mind—your mental self. Immediately following the eight blank lines are some concepts to help jumpstart your thinking.

1._____   5._____

2._____   6._____

3._____   7._____

4._____   8._____

Accurate
Achiever
Action-oriented
Adaptive
Alert
Aggressive
Ambitious
Analytical
Anxious
Assertive
Brave
Calm
Capable
Cautious
Cerebral
Challenger
Composed
Complacent
Competent
Confident
Confrontational
Control

Creative
Critical
Curious
Decisive
Determined
Dislikes Change
Dominating
Driven
Easy-going (relaxed)
Enthusiastic
Energetic
Entrepreneurial
Excelling
Firm
Flair
Flamboyant
Focused
Forthcoming
Goal-oriented
Hard-working
Imagination
Impractical

Indecisive

Independent

Individualist

Indomitable

Innovative

Inquisitive

Inventive

Knowledge

Leader

Learner

Likes challenge

Mentally tough

Motivation

Open book

Open-minded

Optimistic

Orderly

Perfectionistic

Positive

Pragmatic

Precise

Pre-occupied

Purposeful

Rational

Reading

Referee

Relentlessness

Resourceful

Risk-taker

Scattered

Scheduled

Self-assurance

Self-confident

Self-reliant

Self-talk

Slothful

Spirited

Straight-talking

Strong-willed

Stubborn

Success

Suspicious

Takes charge

Teachable

Tenacity

Thoughtful

Troubleshooter

Unrealistic

Vigorous

Vision

Visualization

Vitality

Willful

Work Ethic

Narrow it down to the top four words that best describe your mind—your mental self.

1._____

2._____

3._____

4._____

Now choose the ONE word that epitomizes your mind—your mental self.

1._____

Spirit: Do you feel a relationship to your spiritual origin? Are you able to spend time in meditation? Do you have a relationship with your own inner wisdom, values, beliefs, or intuitive guidance? Do you have moments when you feel at one with everything or part of something more significant? Is nature vital to you?

List eight words that best describe your spirit—your spiritual self. Immediately following the eight blank lines are some concepts to help jumpstart your thinking.

1._____   5._____

2._____   6._____

3._____   7._____

4._____   8._____

Accepting	Iconoclast
Advocate	**Identity**
Agnostic	Insightful
Anarchist	Inspirational
Atheist	Integrity
Avaricious	Interpersonal
Awareness	Investigator
Beauty	Justice
Caring	Karma
Certitude	Love
Committed	Loving-kindness
Compassion	Loyal
Courage	Meaning
Cunning	Mediator
Defender	**Modesty**
Discipline	Motivator
Doubter	Nature
Equality	Nihilism
Existentialism	**Open-hearted**
Fearful	Patience
Freedom	Peacemaker
Generous	Principled
Harmony	Protector
Helper	Purpose
Holistic	Reformer
Humility	Reliable

Responsible	Significance
Ritual	Skeptic
Self-controlled	Supporter
Self-honesty	Sweetness
Self-indulgent	Tradition
Sensitive	Trustworthy
Servant	Truth
Service	Wisdom

Narrow it down to the top four words that best describe your spirit—your spiritual self.

1._____

2._____

3._____

4._____

Now choose the ONE word that epitomizes your spirit—your spiritual self.

1._____

Soul: Are you in touch with your feelings and able to express them appropriately? Do you allow yourself to feel the full range of emotions—fear, sadness, anger, as well as love and joy—or do you find that certain emotions make you uncomfortable? Are you able to set appropriate boundaries with people? Can you relate to others in a close, intimate way?[66]

List eight words that best describe your soul—your emotional self. Immediately following the eight blank lines are some concepts to help jumpstart your thinking.

1._____   5._____

2._____   6._____

3._____   7._____

4._____   8._____

Affection   Easygoing
Agreeable   Eccentricity
Anxious   Empathy
Appreciative   Enthusiast
Arrogant   Easygoing
Bold   Engaging
Charming   Entertainer
Communion   Excited
Complacent   Expressive
Content   Extrovert
Defiant   Fearful
Detached   Fun-loving
Distractible   Group-oriented
Dramatic   Happiness
Dreamer   High-spirited
Dreamy   High-strung

Impatience	Reassuring
Impulsiveness	Rebellious
Intense	Receptive
Intimacy	Relational
Introvert	Reserved
Intuition	Tribal
Isolated	Satisfied
Joyous	Scattered
Lusty	Secretive
Melancholy	Self-absorbed
Mixes easily	Self-aware
Moody	Self-conscious
Non-demanding	Self-pity
Nurturing	Spontaneous
Optimistic	Stable
People-pleasing	Suspicious
Perceptive	Sympathetic
Pessimistic	Temperamental
Playful	Utopian
Possessive	Versatile
Promoter	Withdrawn
Reactive	

Narrow it down to the top four words that best describe your soul—your emotional self.

1._____

2._____

3._____

4._____

Now choose the ONE word that epitomizes your soul—your emotional self.

1._____

Note additional thoughts and feelings and consider how well you currently experience each of the four essentials. Are there any actions you can take toward growth, wholeness, and belonging?

_____

_____

_____

It is invaluable to this process that once you determine your best words—give three people you trust the opportunity to add or dialogue about the words and then rank them in order of importance. This is critical. You need objective and honest, loving and trustworthy input to make your mandala the best possible investment of your time.

3. Piecing Together the Essentials

Now the fun part! Let's piece together the layers into a personal mandala. This is where your unique personality emerges. You can utilize the words you have chosen to represent your essentials. To be the most effective, you must make the mandala your own. A triad may fit better for you such as body, mind, spirit; or a dyad (a group of two) such as mind and body. Use whatever is best for you.

The power of this profound but straightforward tool (and what makes it much more effective than useful assessments such as *Meyers-Briggs, DISC,* and the *Enneagram)* is that it does not attempt to squeeze you into a predetermined box of four to eight narrow categories or numbers. The possibilities of the mandala (especially when you gather outside input from your closest acquaintances) are infinite.

You know yourself better than anyone else. Once you have feedback from trusted friends or family, you can best choose the layers that represent you. Then you add other layers such as compass directions, natural elements, color, seasons, art, and any other symbols that best describe your sense of self.

At first, it might seem intimidating to draw a mandala. But you will find it to be a surprisingly easy project. As you'll see when you start sketching, it is a reflective exercise, and it is not unusual to finish this activity feeling renewed and creative. Let's get started.

Step 7

In Which We Create
A Personal Mandala

The Mandala is a visual representation of our self as a whole—our center, our essentials, and our layers. You will need a pencil, pen, or whatever drawing medium you prefer, a drawing surface, and you may want a ruler and round objects you can trace.

First: Draw a circle and make it large. You will be adding elements and writing in it. Use a compass or a plate as a guide. You can also draw it freehand.

Second: Draw a small circle in the center of your large circle. This represents your center or as Jung calls it, your ego. Place the word from Step 5, item number 1, in that inner circle. The word that best describes your center. I have placed mine there for illustration purposes.

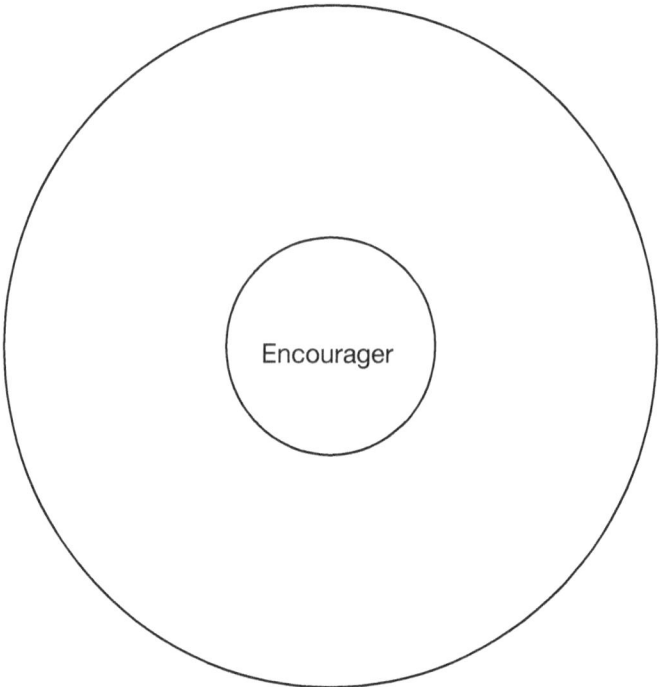

Encourager

Third: Draw one line horizontally in the center of your circle, then another vertically, so that you have four equal quadrants in the circle taking care not to draw in your center circle. If you are utilizing dyads or triads, draw the lines accordingly splitting the circle into two or three equal parts.

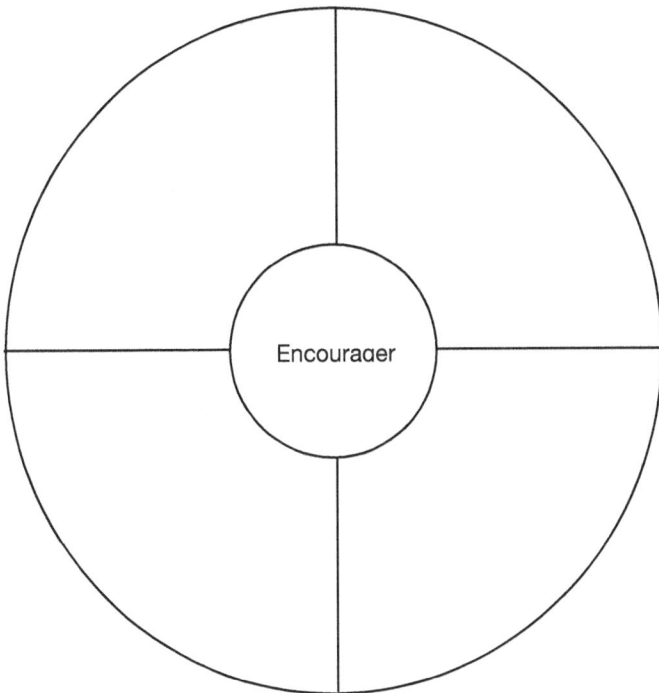

Encourager

Fourth: Label each quadrant with one of the four aspects of your being. Again, if you are utilizing dyads or triads, label the two or three equal parts.

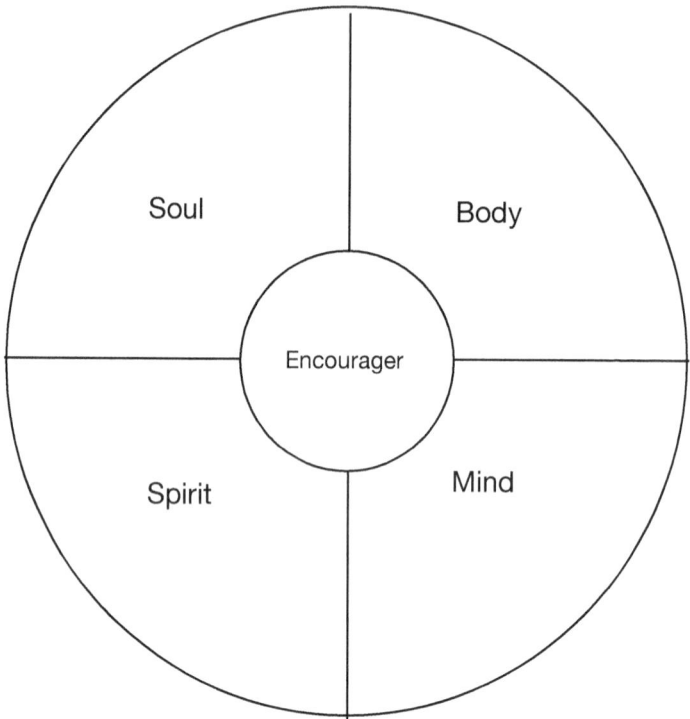

Soul

Body

Encourager

Spirit

Mind

Fifth: Place the word that best describes your body, mind, spirit, and soul from Step 6, number 2 in the appropriate quadrants. I have added mine for illustration purposes.

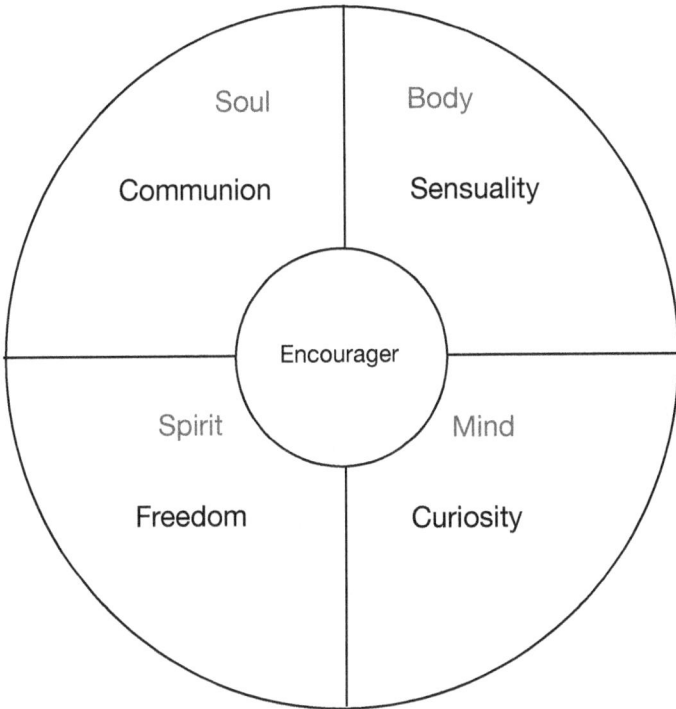

Sixth: Place the sets of the top four words you chose that best describe your body, mind, spirit, and soul from Step 6, number 2. Place them beside or in the appropriate quadrants. I have added mine for illustration purposes.

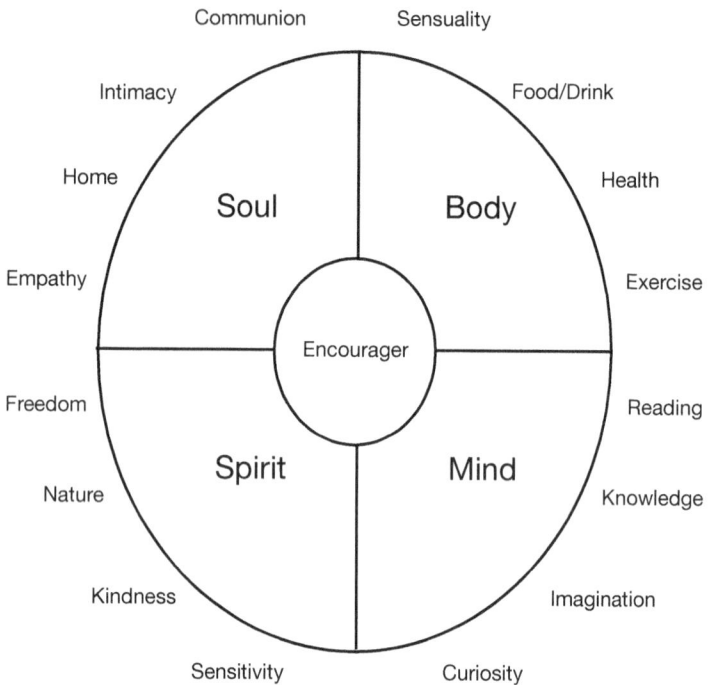

Seventh: Add additional layers of meaning to each of your essentials. Draw the layers on subsequent pages or use a software program to create multiple overlays. Your imagination is the only limit. As you add the layers and symbols—the subtle nuances of who you are will begin to emerge.

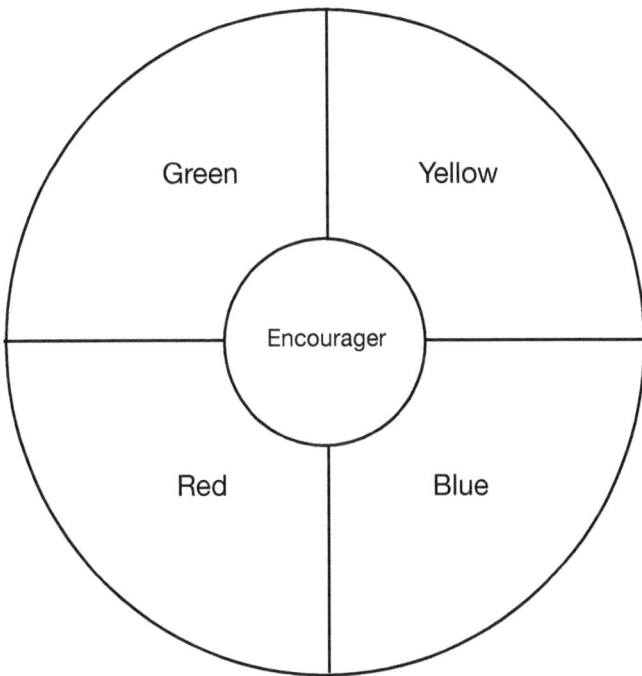

Green

Yellow

Encourager

Red

Blue

Colors—Which color best represents each of your essentials? For example, I use green to describe my body because people have long called me "earthy." Blue depicts my spirit and symbolizes freedom, "blue sky thinking" or "the sky is the limit." Red is for my soul to represent fire and passion, and yellow as a symbol of curiosity for my mind from the movie title about a searching and rebellious personal quest called *I Am Curious—Yellow.*

Creating your personal mandala can be as simple as placing the appropriate words for your center and essentials in a circle with equal divisions similar to the previous illustrations. However, as you add the words for colors, you begin to see the possibilities (as did Carl Jung) of making your mandala a work of art. Some artists have made iterations of their mandalas public, but many people will want to keep their personal mandalas private. I have posted a few iterations of my mandala at *randyelrod.com/resources* to provide inspiration for you.

Four Cardinal Directions—*North, East, South, West.* I list them in the clockwise direction they appear on a Mandala with North at the top. Which direction best represents each of your essentials? The Lakota Indian Tribe views the world in Four Directions. From these come the four winds. The individual meanings of the Four Directions are enhanced by specific colors, and the shape of the cross symbolizes each orientation.

North (Red): North brings the cold, harsh winds of the winter season. These winds are cleansing. They cause the leaves to fall and the earth to rest under a blanket of snow. They symbolize patience and endurance. Generally, this direction stands for hardships and discomfort. Therefore, the north represents trials people endure and the subsequent cleansing they must undergo.

East (Yellow): The direction from which the sun comes. Light dawns in the morning and spreads over the earth. This is the beginning of a new day, and the beginning of understanding because light helps us see things as they are. On a deeper level, east stands for the wisdom that allows people to live purposeful lives.

South (White): Because the southern sky is when the sun is at its highest, this direction stands for warmth and growth. The sun's rays are powerful in drawing life from the earth. It is said the essence of all things comes from the south. Warm and pleasant winds come from that direction.

West (Black): To the west, the sun sets, and the day ends. For this reason, west signifies the end of life. The west sends thunder and rain from its direction. It is the source of water: rain, lakes, streams, and rivers. Nothing can live without water, so the west is vital.[67]

Seasons—*Winter, Spring, Summer, Autumn.* Which season will best represent each essential? For example, I used Winter to express my soul because I have been described as an old soul—as in "Old Man Winter." Autumn represents my body in its present physical age of sixty. Summer symbolizes my spirit because that is the time to shed our clothes and I have often been called a "free spirit." I chose Spring to represent my mind because I wish to be ever renewing and blossoming with knowledge.

A Sense of Place—*Geographical, Psychographical, Ideological, Psychological.* These terms are explained in detail in Step 8.

Symbols—*Yin and Yang, Music, Flowers, Weather, Equality, Peace, Emotions, Graphical Signs, Shapes, Icons, Planets, Greek Gods, etc.* The layers and symbols that can represent your essentials are endless. As you regularly take time to examine your self and create mandalas, you will find it refreshing to encompass new elements to portray your being.

Eighth: Your mandala is taking shape. A beautiful image of your inner self begins to emerge, as you see a visual symbol (a mirror) of your center and your essentials all working together as a cohesive and healthy you. When one of the quadrants splits away (or fragments) from the center and moves away from the other essentials due to past wounds—or grief, loss, betrayal, repression, or control by one of the institutions of life—to some degree, you have become lost from yourself.

That is why regular self-evaluation with the mandala is vital. It provides a visual snapshot of your inner self and the cohesiveness of each aspect to the other. It gives a mirror not only for the soul, but for the body, mind, and spirit as well. Your whole being emerges. If you see signs of fragmentation, you know it is time to take a break and rest, talk to a trusted friend or companion, attend a support group, see a therapist, or any other method that best provides healing and promotes wholeness.

Fragmentation

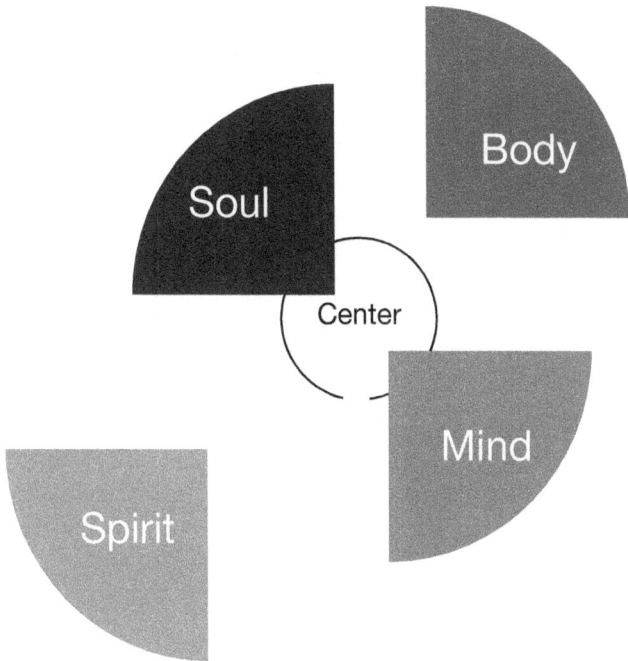

It is important to note that emotional healing (our soul) takes more time than physical healing (our body.) A week-long holiday may provide healing for a tired body, but a long sabbatical may be required for a weary soul.

My soul was fragmented to the point of death by a lifetime of imprisonment to the institutions of life and a desperate need for approval. Therapy, times spent in nature and solitude, and communion with my wife who is also my companion (we'll talk about that vital concept in Step 9), have contributed to my recovery and a new understanding of my essentials and wholeness.

Please know that it has taken over ten years for my soul to begin healing, and to understand and commence congruence with my spirit, mind, and body. Have patience, there is hope.

The mandala has become a powerful tool in the discovery and healing of my self. I have built a 20-foot mandala (aka Native American medicine wheel) of rocks gathered from our land in an area we have designated sacred ground atop the southern ridge of our Appalachian retreat called *Kalien*. I also create mandalas with watercolors.

An Internet search will provide thousands of mandalas for viewing and a springboard for the creation of your own. I encourage you to try it. Find a few pieces of paper and some pencils and crayons and give it a try. The physical elements can add a pleasing tactile experience. However, digital drawing apps allow saving and archiving countless iterations.

Whatever your preference, give it a go. I've found that drawing, coloring, or painting my mandala has been healing and refreshing and the layers and symbols have opened my eyes to previously hidden nuances of my self. I'm surprised by how often it changes. Ah yes, I am growing again. I am becoming who I am. I am alive. I have hope.

Now that we are beginning to understand the journey to finding ourselves (a sense of self), we can now go about the task of finding others (a sense of place). A path of discovery to a new and better tribe.

III.Finding Others

Randy Elrod

Step 8

In Which We Seek To Understand Tribal Relationships and A Sense of Place

Most of us have been fortunate to be part of a tribe at least once in our lives. Maybe you felt that sense of belonging on your wedding day when family and friends gathered to celebrate your marriage. Or when your favorite football team won the Super Bowl, and at your party you cheered, high-fived, and bonded with friends over beer and nachos.

Perhaps you've sensed it in church, in your book group, in yoga class, or at a family reunion. Maybe you've felt it on girl's night out or when you rushed a fraternity or at an annual conference that became like family.

All of us crave being part of something bigger than ourselves. By nature, we are tribal, and back in cave dweller days, tribal culture was necessary for human survival. But increasingly, we have become disconnected from our tribe.

It could be that we grew disillusioned with our church family, or relocated far away from our neighborhood. Perhaps we gradually divided politically, or grew apart from our family, or went through a divorce. In today's highly mobile society there are many reasons for the loss of belonging.

We know that new and better people are out there somewhere—but we feel alone and disconnected from them. We seek them, but they keep eluding us. We are not sure how to find them. Without a tribe, we may wind up feeling isolated, depressed, spiritually disconnected, and even sick.

Models of friendship show two main factors impact our choice and pursuit of potential tribe members: *a sense of self* (individual) and *a sense of place* (environment). Individual factors include such effects as approachability, social skills, self-disclosure, similarity, and closeness. Environmental factors include forces such as geography, psychographics, (activities, interests, and opinions), demographics, and ideology.[68]

Research continues to support our preferences for tribe members who we believe to be similar to ourselves and who have personalities that we enjoy being around. Choosing harmonious relationships decrease the possibility of interpersonal conflict.

The Power of Tribal Relationships

Dr. Lissa Rankin recounts this intriguing story about the town of Roseto, Pennsylvania.[69] Back in the 1960s, if you had stumbled upon the small town of Italian immigrants, you would have seen people returning from work at the end of the day, strolling along the village's main street, stopping to gossip with the neighbors, and maybe sharing a glass of wine before heading home to change into dinner clothes.

You'd see women gathering together in communal kitchens, preparing classic Italian feasts, while men pushed tables together in anticipation of the nightly ritual that gathered the community together over heaping piles of pasta, Italian sausage, meatballs fried in lard, and free-flowing vino.

As a community of new immigrants, surrounded by English and Welsh neighbors who turned up their noses at the Italians, the people of Roseto had to look out for each other. Multi-generational homes were the norm. During the week, everyone went to the same workplace, and on Sundays, everyone went to church together. Neighbors wandered in and out of each other's kitchens regularly, and holidays were joyously celebrated communally.

The people of Roseto took care of each other. Nobody in Roseto was left to struggle through life alone. The town was living proof of the power of the clan. And while they smoked, drank booze every night, and ate junk food, the people of Roseto had half the risk of death by a heart attack as the rest of the country. It was not because of genetics, better doctors, or something in their water supply—researchers ultimately concluded that love, intimacy, and being part of a tribe protected their health.

John Bruhn, a sociologist, recalls, "There was no suicide, no alcoholism, no drug addiction, and little crime. They didn't have anyone on welfare. Then we looked at peptic ulcers. They didn't have any of those either. These people were dying of old age. That's it."[70]

Then Everything Changed

As time went on, the younger generation wasn't so thrilled about life in Roseto, which to them seemed immune to modernization. When the young people went off to study at college, they brought back to Roseto new ideas, new dreams, and new people. Italian-Americans started marrying non-Italians. The children strayed from the church, joined country clubs, and moved into single-family suburban houses with fences and pools.

With these changes, the multi-generational homes disbanded and the community lifestyle shifted gears from nightly celebrations to more of the typical "every man for himself" philosophy that fueled the neighboring communities. The neighbors who would regularly drop in for casual visits started phoning each other to schedule appointments. The evening rituals of adults singing songs while children played with marbles and jacks turned into nights in front of the television.

In 1971, when heart attack rates in other parts of the country were dropping because of widespread adoption of healthier diets and regular exercise programs, Roseto had its first heart attack death in someone younger than age 45. Over the next decade, heart disease rates in Roseto doubled. The incidence of high blood pressure tripled, and the number of strokes increased. Sadly, by the end of the 1970s, the number of fatal heart attacks in Roseto had risen to the national average.

As it turns out, human beings nourish each other, even more than Italian food and wine, and the health of our being reflects this. Positive tribal relationships benefit our body, mind, spirit, and soul—our physical, emotional, spiritual, and mental health. Belonging is a big deal. Not only is it human nature to crave intimacy and community, but it's also preventative medicine.

To summarize, a tribal relationship is an association between people that may range in duration from brief to long-term. Like people, tribal relationships change and grow; they may either improve or grow apart over time. The relationship between two people can be based on various factors—love, commonalities, business, or any other context that requires two people to interact.

A Sense of Place

As we continue the individual quest for a *sense* (or perception) *of self*, it behooves us to embark upon an environmental search—our *sense of place*. The term sense of place has become a buzzword used to justify everything from a mystical appreciation of a home in the country to the selling of large suburban homesites.

The truth is that few Americans have a single "sense of place" like the residents of Roseto. We are likely to have relationships over the years with several places as the institutions of life uproot and relocate us. According to the United States Census Bureau, a typical American will move 11.7 times during their life.[71]

Let's examine how our body, mind, spirit, and soul view the places that look and feel like home to us. On the mandala, I label them geographical, demographical, psychographical, and ideological. These are the cultural preconceptions that shape the way we respond to an environment. They make up our sense of place.

We bring a whole set of biases to the many places we live in. These assumptions shape the way we respond to a place. In some measure, we attempt to reshape the location to fit our preconceptions. Further complicating our understanding of a sense of place is that in contemporary society, it is possible to have more than one relationship with a single area, and those relationships are likely to change over time.

Let's relate those connections to the four essentials of our selves. The relationships may be described in our context as follows.

Geographical/Physical/Body

This aspect relates to our family history and our genealogy—being born in, and growing up in a place. The geographical element of a sense of place develops over time and can prove extremely strong. When we speak of "going home" it usually means geographically. These strong and enduring relationships are attachments based on our personal history with a location. They are characterized by a strong sense of identification and a long-term residence.

In geographical relationships, a sense of place is a physical part of our history. They require time to develop and are most powerful in areas you have spent significant time and have extensive experiences and memories. These become part of your individual (sense of self) and environmental (sense of place) identity.

Geographical relationships sound like this statement: "This place *looks* and *smells* like home."

Demographical/Mental/Mind

This aspect describes the statistical data relating to the people within it. Americans hail from areas as diverse as the rural south, the academic northeast, and the free-spirited Western states. A defining characteristic of the demographic relationship is a rational choice, the ability to choose a place with the best possible combination of desirable features.

Demographic relationships have little or nothing to do with personal history. Because they are founded on your list of desirable traits, demographic relationships typically result from dissatisfaction with a former community and the quest to find a more desirable place. This relationship is based on the match between the attributes of a location and what you think is a "perfect" place. Not surprisingly your perception of the ideal community changes across the life-cycle.

Demographical relationships sound like this statement: "These people *reflect* my worldview."

Ideological/Spiritual/Spirit

This relationship is about ethical living according to your moral guidelines and responsibility to a place. The ground rules may be sacred or secular. For some, this comes in the form of religious or spiritual teachings, and for others, it is a secular ethic of responsibility. The ideological relationship embodies a profound sense of belonging. In spiritual terms, it often feels mystical. Ideological connections are founded on values and beliefs about how we should relate to physical places. The defining characteristic of ideological relationships is a well-articulated ideology about *how* to live in a place.

Ideological relationships sound like this statement: "These people *believe* as I do."

Psychographical/Emotional/Soul

Psychographics is a methodology used to describe psychological attributes such as personality, values, opinions, attitudes, interests, and lifestyles.[72] These are our emotional and intangible feelings that form a sense of belonging. It encompasses our traditions relating to a place through stories. Psychographics include family histories—and social, political and fictional narratives. These aspects are often the most robust and most enduring relationships and create an emotional attachment to a place.

Psychographical relationships sound like this statement: "This place *feels* like home."

A Personal Journey

Perhaps this story will help illustrate our tribal relationships and sense of place. I was born and grew up in the Appalachian mountains of Tennessee. Geographically, it was verdant, mountainous and remote. Demographically, the racial makeup of my Tennessee county was 99% white and was named an "extreme whitopia" in Rich Benjamin's book, *Searching for Whitopia*.[73] The median income for the county was $16,468. Two out of every ten people lived below the poverty line.

Psychographically, Whitwell was a place of uneducated, hard-working people, many of them coal miners. People grew old before their time, and communities were clannish and closed minded. The people were quiet, even-tempered, and kept to themselves.

Ideologically, it was predominantly Baptist, ultra-conservative, and 80/20 mix of Republicans to Democrat.

At the age of 26, I moved to a South Florida condo in the idyllic beach town of Stuart, a few miles north of Jupiter Island. Demographically, the racial makeup was far more diverse. 86% White, 8% Latino, 5% African American. The median income was $52,622, with adjacent Jupiter Island boasting a staggering median household income of $248,750. The culture shock was overwhelming and at times humiliating, but it changed my life for the better.

Psychographically, Stuart was a place of educated, wealthy people, many of them retired. People acted younger than their age, and communities were diverse and open-minded. The people were loud, obnoxious, and full of themselves. One in ten people spoke Spanish. Ideologically it was predominantly non-Christian and Catholic, liberal, and a 60/40 mix of Republicans to Democrats.

Even though Stuart was radically different from the place I grew up, in many ways it still *feels* like home. I found it to be a stimulating and creative environment. The diversity and open-mindedness were complementary to the person I was becoming. My children lived their earliest days in the South Florida town—one was born there—and much of our early nuclear family history and stories originated there. Great friendships were formed and some last to this day. I've often said the fondest memories of my early life were in Stuart.

After over 14 years in Florida, I moved back to a spacious house in the historic district of Franklin, Tennessee on Main Street. Demographically, the racial makeup of the county was 91% White, 5% African American, 3% Latino. Williamson County has a per capita income of $104,367, which ranks as *Forbes Magazine's* 7th most affluent county in America. To say this was NOT like moving back home to Whitwell is an understatement.

Psychographically, Franklin was a place of educated, wealthy people, many of them in the entertainment industry. People acted their age, and communities were cloistered and narrow-minded. The people were moderately loud, confident, and entitled. Almost everyone speaks English. Ideologically it was highly religious and predominantly Baptist and Methodist, conservative, and a 70/30 mix of Republicans to Democrats. Most of the friendships formed there dissolved after my mid-life crisis and subsequent divorce. My world-view had changed, and Franklin did not reflect my new ideology. The people as a whole did not *believe* as I did.

After a divorce from my wife of thirty-two years and living eleven years in the conservative enclave of Franklin, I moved to an 800-square-foot loft apartment in downtown Austin, Texas. Demographically, the racial makeup was 49% White, 35% Latino, 8% African American, and 7% Asian. Austin was by far the most racially diverse place of my life. Travis County has a per capita income of $67, 116. I found the rapidly growing inner-city exhilarating, but it was a long distance from family.

Psychographically, Austin was a place of highly-educated, wealthy people, many of them in the tech industry. People acted their age, and communities were urban and open-minded. The people were moderately loud, confident, and proud to be called weird. Four in ten people speak Spanish. Ideologically it was somewhat religious and predominantly Catholic, liberal, and a 70/30 mix of Democrats to Republicans. But geographically it "looked" and "smelled" too different to feel like home to me.

I remarried and eventually succumbed to a longing to go back "home" again. We purchased a remote fifty-four-acre farm in the Appalachian foothills seventy miles (as the crow flies) from my childhood home. Demographically, Smith County, Tennessee has a racial makeup that is 96% White, 2% Latino, and 2% African American. The median income is $23,015. We still have a country home there as of this writing.

Psychographically, Gordonsville is a place of high school educated, working class people, many of them farmers. People act and look older than their age, and communities are rural and close-minded. The people are quiet, even-tempered, and mind their own business. Everyone speaks English. Ideologically it is religious and predominantly Baptist, conservative, and an 80/20 mix of Republicans to Democrats.

After spending three years building a spacious country home, a guest cabin, and an artist cabin, we settled into our new life where the dirt smelled like home and the rhythm of the four seasons brought back waves of nostalgia. It provided a place to forgive, heal, and explore my sense of self. But after two more years, it was increasingly evident that in this season of life our sense of place had changed.

Due to the diversity of the many places we had lived, and after evaluating the essentials and layers of our being, we found it imperative to find a new and better place that fit us psychographically, demographically and ideologically.

We began the search for a second home in Knoxville, Tennessee; Asheville, North Carolina; and Greenville, South Carolina. But these cities did not entirely fit our new sense of self and place. A relationship of wholeness to our new residence seemed crucial to us, especially if we were to continue our search for a new and better tribe.

In the spring of 2018, after a long search, we bought a second home—a beach cottage in Dunedin, Florida. Demographically, it has a racial makeup of 75% White, 11% African American, 10% Latino, and 4% Asian. It has a median income of $46,310.

Psychographically, Dunedin is a place of educated, forward-thinking people, many of them are business owners. People act and look younger than their age, and communities are eclectic and open-minded. The people are moderately loud, even-tempered, and communal. Most speak English. Ideologically it is secular and predominantly irreligious, leaning liberal, and a 60/40 mix of Democrats to Republicans.

Over the years my wife had repeatedly said she would never move back to her home state of Florida, but as we strolled the streets of the whimsical and off-beat downtown of Dunedin, we both felt an overwhelming sense of place. We used our mandala to explore the essential aspects we desired in a new environment. A place with the potential to regain belonging and to find new and better tribe members.

The growing need for belonging prompted the decision to move our official residence to Dunedin. The demographic, ideological, and psychographic diversity of this town has already provided new relationships and given us a profound sense of belonging that we can't explain.

Geographically, the Appalachian farm in Tennessee physically looks (the mountains, the forests, the four seasons) and smells (the dirt, the flora, and the fauna) like home to me. But for my wife, the beach cottage in Dunedin is a geographical fit, it looks (the beach, the water, and the eternal sunshine) and smells (the surf, the flora, and the fauna) like home to her.

But for both of us, the Dunedin demographic (age and racial diversity), the psychographic (open-mindedness, equality for all), and the ideology (leaning liberal and irreligious) are mentally, emotionally, and spiritually congruent with the essentials of our mind, spirit, and soul for this season of our lives.

Although every place has its unique influence for how we relate to it, it is important to remember that our *relationships with* and *attachments to* places are interrelated to our personal history and to the essentials of our being. How I feel in one place is influenced by the positive and negative feelings I have for other areas.

A sense of place is an experience created by the personal essentials a person brings to it combined with the environmental setting. In other words, to some degree, our sense of self guides our sense of place in this world, and ideally, they do not exist independent of each other.

Congruent tribal and spatial relationships benefit our whole being—our body, mind, spirit, and soul. A cohesive sense of self and sense of space can enhance our physical, mental, spiritual, and emotional health much like the citizens of Roseto in its early days.

Some Questions To Ask About Your Sense of Place

1. Is the place where you live now remarkably similar, somewhat similar, unlike, or very unlike the town of Roseto?

2. What is the geography of your birthplace? Growing up place? Current home? Favorite place?

3. What are the demographics of your birthplace? Growing up place? Current home? Favorite place?*

4. What is the racial makeup of your birthplace? Growing up place? Current home? Favorite place?

5. What is the median income of your birthplace? Growing up place? Current home? Favorite place?

6. What are the psychographics of your birthplace? Growing up place? Current home? Favorite place?

7. How do people look and act in your birthplace? Growing up place? Current home? Favorite place?

8. How would you describe your birthplace? Growing up place? Current home? Favorite place? Open-minded or close-minded.

9. How would you describe your birthplace? Growing up place? Current home? Favorite place? Traditional, eclectic, or off-beat.

10. What is the average education level of your birthplace? Growing up place? Current home? Favorite place?

11. What is the political party of your birthplace? Growing up place? Current home? Favorite place?

12. What is the predominant religion of your birthplace? Growing up place? Current home? Favorite place?

13. How do the geographical, demographical, ideological, and psychographical aspects of your current home line up with your essentials from Step 6? Does it *look* and *smell* like home? Do the people *reflect* your worldview? Do the people *believe* as you do? Does it *feel* like home?

14. What essentials should I look for in my next place of residence?

15. Which essentials should be non-negotiable in my next place of residence?

I would strongly suggest writing your own personal journey —a detailed and chronological account of the places you've lived and how they impacted your being. It is an eye-opening exercise.

*An excellent resource for demographics and ideology research is: https://www.bestplaces.net

Step 9

In Which We Examine Four Categories of Tribal Relationships

There are many valuable things in life, and a tribe is one of the most important. To live life without the experience of belonging is a life without living. Tribal relationships are essential to our success and well being.

Grouping tribal relationships into categories help as we seek to find a new and better tribe. We place tribe members into categories because all connections are not equal. The four types are fans, acquaintances, friends, and companions.

Robin Dunbar, a University of Oxford anthropologist and psychologist, was trying to understand why primates devote so much time and effort to grooming. In the investigative process, he chanced upon a far more intriguing application for his research.

His *Social Brain Hypothesis* holds that primates have large brains because they live in socially complex societies: the larger the group, the larger the brain. Thus, from the size of an animal's neocortex, you could theoretically predict the group size for that animal.

Looking at his grooming data, Dunbar made the mental leap to humans. "We also had humans in our data set so it occurred to me to look to see what size group that relationship might predict for humans."[74] Dunbar did the math, using a ratio of neocortical volume to total brain volume and mean group size, and came up with a number.

Judging from the size of a human brain, the number of people the average person can have meaningful relationships with is a hundred and fifty. Anything beyond that is too complicated to handle at optimal processing levels. For the last twenty-two years, Dunbar has been "unpacking and exploring" what that number means—and whether our ever-expanding social networks have done anything to change it.

In recent years, Dunbar has taken his idea further by taking into account the emotional closeness between individuals. This has led him to the concept of **Dunbar Layers**: *that an individual's group of 150 contacts is layered according to the strength of emotional ties.*

Individuals, he says, generally have up to five people in the closest layer. The next closest layer contains an additional 10, the one beyond that an extra 35, and the final group another 100. Cumulatively, the segments comprise around five, fifteen, fifty, and 150 people.[75] Every person is different, and large variabilities can occur between individuals. These numbers are not set in concrete.

Dunbar discovered that the number grows and decreases according to a precise formula, roughly a "rule of three." The ranges are 50-100 people that you would call *casual* friends. Next, are the 30-50 people you would refer to as *good* friends—perhaps the people you'd invite to a group dinner. You see them often, but not so much that you consider them to be true intimates.

Then there's the circle of 10-15 *close* friends that you can turn to for sympathy when you need it, the ones you can confide in about most things.

The most intimate Dunbar number range, 4-5, is your support group. These are your *best* friends (and can often include family members).

On the flip side, group ranges can in some rare examples possibly extend to 300-500 in the *acquaintance* level, and 1,000-1500, the absolute limit for the people whom you can put a name to a face. There is evidence that ranges may vary based upon the extrovert and introverted temperament.

While the group sizes are relatively stable, their composition can be fluid. Your five today may not be your five next week; people drift among layers and sometimes fall out of them altogether. With that information in mind, let's look at the four categories of tribe members.

When looking at these first two ranges that number in the hundreds and thousands, it is crucial to reiterate that Dunbar says humans do seem to have a natural limit to the number of *meaningful* relationships they can have. This number is about 150.

Fans (Dunbar Range: 1000-1500)

I call the first category of tribal relationship *fans*. To clarify, when someone is a fan, they like what they know about you and are peripherally interested. They are only concerned with relatively minor, irrelevant, or superficial aspects of your life. Fans like what they occasionally see you *do*, but they do not know who you *are*. They are the people for whom you can probably put a name to a face. Most fans do not live in your physical world.

Digital fans include the majority of your social networks. *Facebook* calls them friends, *Twitter* and *Instagram* call them followers, *LinkedIn* calls them connections, and *YouTube* calls them subscribers.

Performers, speakers, authors, artists, celebrities, athletes, politicians, and entertainers usually have *physical* fans as well.

Remember, the group sizes are relatively stable, but their composition can be fluid. Your 1500 today may not be your 1500 next week; fans come and go with the wind and having essentials in common is mostly irrelevant.

Acquaintances (Dunbar Range: 300-500)

The second category of tribal relationship is an *acquaintance*. An acquaintance likes you for *what you do* and can be marginally interested. These people are the most likely predecessors to a casual friendship. What they know about your life is merely an observation. Usually, these are the types of tribe members that you physically see in school, at work, local hangouts, or a place that you frequent.

The two types of acquaintances in our quest for a new and better tribe can be understood as *casual* and *cordial*.

Casual acquaintances usually give you a slight smile and greeting. These are the people that know of your existence. The bartender at the local brewery could be a casual acquaintance and will likely nod and wave if she recognizes you outside of work.

The *cordial acquaintance* may be someone that sits in a class that you share. It could even be a friend of a friend, one that you see somewhat frequently, but conversations rarely go into depth. The owner at the local bookstore could be a cordial acquaintance and will undoubtedly say a word of greeting and shake hands if they run into you outside of the store.

Remember, the group sizes are relatively stable, but their composition can be fluid. Your 500 today may not be your 500 next week; acquaintances drift among layers and sometimes fall out of them altogether. You may share one or more physical or mental essentials in common with a cordial acquaintance.

It is crucial to understand that lesser known tribe members—fans and acquaintances—are not bad. They have the highest potential to become friends and new members of your tribe. Many of our relationships are accidental. It is easier to stay on the surface with acquaintances, even cordial ones; these relationships allow us to breathe and deal with the practicalities of life. But sometimes we crave a bit of depth.

Since we cannot love someone unless we know them, and since we only come to know them after a significant period, true friendship and companionship will be rare. The important thing is to develop friendships that matter.

Friends (Dunbar Range: 5-150)

The third category for tribal relationships is a *friend*. A friend likes you for *who you are*. They are interested in the real you. These people are the most likely candidates for a new and better tribe. What they know about your life is primarily based on the amount of time they spend with you. Usually, these are the types of tribe members that you live, work, or play with. Friends feel they know you.

Thinkers throughout history have had much to say about friendship. The German philosopher Friedrich Nietzsche suggests that our first question about a potential friend should be: "Can they walk? Can they stand up straight, carry their own weight, cover ground, and make progress?" He felt many people do not.

Aristotle's impact can still be felt in many disciplines, and one of his most enduring observations relates to friendship. He saw friendship as one of the real joys of life and thought that a life well-lived must include meaningful and lasting friendships. In his book *Nicomachean Ethics*,[76] he wrote that friendship was "one soul in two bodies."

He further explains that to be an genuine friendship, it should have the following attributes: "To be friends, therefore, men must feel goodwill for each other, that is, wish for each other's good, and be aware of each other's goodwill."

His opinion was that friends hold a mirror up to each other; through that mirror, they can see each other in ways that would not otherwise be accessible to them, and it is this (reciprocal) mirroring that helps them improve as persons.

Friendship is a theme that permeates American essayist Henry David Thoreau's writings. He tells us that "No word is oftener on the lips of men than Friendship, and indeed no thought is more familiar to their aspirations."[77]

We have considered the thoughts of Nietzsche, Aristotle, and Thoreau as they have weighed in on friendship. They represent some of the greatest minds in history. But perhaps the most powerful voice to speak about friendship in our time is the author and speaker Brené Brown, a research professor at the University of Houston who has spent the past two decades studying courage, vulnerability, shame, and empathy.

She says, "authentic friends are the ones you can share your vulnerability and shame with. Show me a person who can listen to a friend and not try to fix their problem but just listen to them and be there for them. Show me a person who can sit quietly with a friend who shares this vulnerability and still love them the way they are, and I'll show you companions who are courageous and have done their work."

"When we're looking for compassion, we need someone who is deeply rooted, is able to bend and, most of all embrace us for our strengths and struggles. We need to honor our effort by sharing it with someone who has *earned* the right to hear it. When we're looking for compassion, it's about connecting with the *right person* at the *right time* about the *right issue*."

Brené Brown calls them "move-a-body friends." She recounts, "A year or two ago, my good friend called, and as soon as I said, 'Hello!' she said, "'You're a friend who would move a body.' I could tell by her voice that she was serious. I lowered my voice and whispered, 'What does that mean?'"

"She said that one of her sister's close friends had called her sister and asked for help to move her mom. The friend's mother, who was apparently only invited to visit once a year, struggled with alcoholism. When my friend's sister's friend came home from work, her mother was passed out drunk on the sofa. It was 3 o'clock in the afternoon, and the kids would be busting through the front door any minute. She called because she physically needed help moving her mother."

Brené says she let out a deep sigh and said, "Yes. You could definitely call me." Her friend then said one of the kindest things that anyone has ever said to her. "I'd call you because you would come right away, give me a hug, never look judgmental or disapproving or disgusted. And then you'd say, 'Let's do this.' The next day, when you saw my mom at the park or the soccer game, you'd be kind and respectful. Most of all, it would never cross my mind to say something to you like 'Please don't tell anyone.' You don't do that."

Brené Brown says she thought about that conversation for days. "I thought about how lucky I am to have a couple of move-a-body friends in my life. I thought about how crazy it is that most of us can steamroll over these friends while we work to win the approval and acceptance of people who don't matter in our lives—people whom we'd *never* call when we were in a real struggle. When we're in the shame storm."

The four types of friends in our quest for a new and better tribe can be understood as *casual, good, close* and *best.*

Casual Friends—People (the number can average around eighty) with whom you have meaningful but perhaps not intimate connections. Those you would invite to a large party.

Good Friends—Robin Dunbar says this list should ideally be around fifty—perhaps the people you'd invite to a group dinner or a wedding. You see them often, but not enough to consider them true intimates.

Close Friends—The circle of ten to fifteen that you can turn to for sympathy when you need it, the ones you can confide in about most things.

Best Friends—The four to five people who are your intimates and close support group. This list often includes family members.

Companions (Dunbar Range: 1-2)

The fourth type of tribal relationship is a *companion.* One or two people which may include your life partner, perhaps a family member, a muse, or the closest friend you have on earth.

"Companions, I need," Nietzsche wrote, "and living ones—not dead companions or corpses I carry wherever I go. But living companions I need who follow me because they wish to follow themselves—and to the places whither I wish to go."[78] *Companions* love you despite knowing the best and worst you have to offer.

The word *companion* ultimately comes from the Latin *com* ("with") and *panis* ("bread, food"). You may be a companion to someone without physically dining with that person, but etymologically you are sharing a meal with them. The word literally means a mate or match for something, and in our context, a companion should share a majority of your essentials, and at best they complement all of them. They are the rarest of companions. I call them *wholemates.*

We tend to be skeptical of what is called the "soulmate" view of friendship: the idea that finding a companion is about finding one's soul in the other. But could it be that to find a true companion we must seek "wholemates"? A *wholemate* is a person that shares aspects of not only our soul—but our body, mind, and spirit as well.

A companion accompanies, guides, and gives support as both of you mutually attempt to understand and improve your true selves. In that sense, companionship is about *wholemates.* Perhaps it's not about finding them ready-made, but it is about gradually becoming *wholemates* for each other.

These relationships require time and intention, but when they blossom, they do so with trust, admiration, and awe. They bring with them some of the sweeter joys that life has to offer.

The French philosopher Montaigne thought this type of companionship was rare. He acknowledges to have found only one proper companion in his life: Etienne de La Boétie and he were able to enjoy this priceless relationship only four brief years. They met as adults and death took Montaigne's soulmate (perhaps his *wholemate*) early. It was an irreplaceable loss.

After La Boétie's death (in 1563), Montaigne didn't feel the desire to find a substitute for his dead friend. Perhaps the reason was that Montaigne knew intuitively that such a deep bond could happen only a few times in a lifetime. In an attempt to describe the nature of his friendship with La Boétie, Montaigne concludes with his famous expression: "If a man should importune me to give a reason why I lov'd him; I find it could no otherwise be exprest, than by making answer: because it was he, because it was I."

True companionship takes time and trust to build. *Companions depend on mutual growth.* We're much more likely to connect at this level with someone when we've seen them at their worst and watched them grow—or if we've endured mutual hardship with them. These relationships are in-depth, intimate, beneficial, and pleasurable.

When you respect a person and care for them, you gain joy from spending time with them. If they're a good enough person to warrant such a relationship, there's utility there, too. They help maintain your mental and emotional health.

The following words express what we all want deep down. We feel ourselves beloved when we know that our friends see us for who we are and loves what they see.

And did you get what
you wanted from this life, even so?
I did.
And what did you want?
To call myself beloved, to feel myself
beloved on the earth.

— *Late Fragment* Raymond Carver[79]

Friends love each other for who they are, for their true selves. Because this love is based on becoming who we are, the friendship is enduring. Imperfect associations, on the other hand, arise and die quickly, because they are based on impermanent things (what we do): beauty, or wealth, or shared experiences. When one or both parties cease to find the connections useful, the companionship ceases as well.

A relationship has to be *about* something. People are best friends or companions because they do things together —they are joined in some "shared aspects of self." It takes time. People spend time together because they need each other and they like each other. They need each other for the "necessities of life."

Companions care *more* about benefiting each other than about helping themselves. They love each other for who they are because they see the thing they care most about—shared essentials.

Whatever we believe to be the meaning of life —*that* is the goal we desire to pursue with our friends and companions. We see in each other shared aspects of the wholeness of life. To love my companion's self is not merely to love certain personality traits, but to love—and to share—that person's understanding of who that person is becoming.

Companions love each other for their own sake, but implicit in that love is a unity of purpose. They are united by common essentials. Just as a football team becomes successful when all its members set aside their own concerns and pursue the goals of the group, true companions single-mindedly pursue *individuation* together.

Companions help each other in the pursuit of wholeness and guard each other's self more carefully than they would each other's property. They have true companionship, because they "wish for what is just and advantageous, and seek it in common."[80]

Family

Family members can fit into any category. Assign them a group as you would any other person. This exercise can be eye-opening if we realize many of our family members are only acquaintances at best. Those with a close-knit family may have them designated as close friends or even in rare cases, as companions. The time-worn cliche is appropriate, "Friends are the family we get to choose."

Make a List of Your Former Tribe

Find a journal and list everyone you can remember from your former tribe in no particular order or category. This will include digital and physical fans; casual and cordial acquaintances; casual, good, close, and best friends; and companions. Do this over some time as the list will continue to grow as you think of additional names.

In this divisive and fragmented time, when many things have lost their value, we need true friendships—relationships that are beautiful and deep in difficult seasons. It is entirely possible that some former tribe members will transition to our new (and better) tribe. Some rare people can love unconditionally and will remain vital tribe members no matter what. A few others may have difficulty, but with time and effort on both parts, they will hang in there with you. There may be ups and downs, but it is possible with time to become even stronger friends than before. For more about this, see Bonus Step #14 *Don't Throw All Former Tribe Members Out With The Bath Water.*

If we are healthy, and we are growing—I outgrew my marriage *and* my religion in a span of a few short years—it is normal (albeit, painful) that friendships grow apart as we move in different ways. As winter vanishes into spring, a long friendship, marriage, or community may fade away.

After you have compiled the names of former tribe members, methodically go down the list and say, "_____(name), thanks and blessings for what you have contributed to my life. Farewell and so long."

This exercise may be challenging and emotional, but the letting go will have an enormous benefit on the journey forward. I took an additional step and made a copy of the list and held a fire ceremony (instructions to do your own ritual can be found at randyelrod.com/resources) and burned the paper signifying a "letting go" as I thanked them once again for being a part of my past life, and I offered forgiveness to those who had wronged me.

Make a List of Your Current Tribe

Now list everyone you can put a name to a face. This will include digital and physical fans; casual and cordial acquaintances; casual, good, close, and best friends; and companions. List them in no particular order or category at first.

Please Note: I made both former and current lists at the same time. At first, my current tribe was tiny, but as I considered anyone whose face I could name, the list began to grow gradually, and I was surprised that eventually, the list had as many people as the former tribe. Don't be discouraged if that is not the case for you at this time. I have been on this journey to find a new and better tribe for over eight years.

When you feel right about your list, assign a category for each name. I used "F" for fans, "A" for an acquaintance, "FR" for friends, and "C" for companions. This will prepare you for the next list. Please note: I have skipped listing casual friends for brevity's sake.

Make a List of Your *Good* Friends

Don't worry if there are only a few. As you continue this journey, the list will grow. Robin Dunbar says this list should ideally be around fifty—perhaps the people you'd invite to a group dinner or a wedding. You see them often, but not enough that you consider them to be true intimates.

Remember, your thirty or fifty today may not be your thirty to fifty next week; people drift among layers and sometimes fall out of them altogether.

1._____   4._____

2._____   5._____

3._____   6._____

7._____

8._____

9._____

10._____

11._____

12._____

13._____

14._____

15._____

16._____

17._____

18._____

19._____

20._____

21._____

22._____

23._____

24._____

25._____

25._____

26._____

27._____

28._____

29._____

30._____

(31)._____

(32)._____

(33)._____

(34)._____

(35)._____

(36)._____

(37)._____

(38)._____

(39)._____

(40)._____

(41)._____

(42)._____

(43)._____

(44)._____

(45)._____

(46)._____

(47)._____

(48)._____   (50)._____

(49)._____

Make a List of Your *Close* Friends

The second type of friend is your *close* friends, the circle of ten to fifteen that you can turn to for sympathy when you need it, the ones you can confide in about most things.

Write out a list of your close friends. Again, don't worry if there are only a few. As you continue this journey, your list will grow. Remember, your ten to fifteen today may not be your ten or fifteen next week; people drift among layers and sometimes fall out of them altogether.

1._____   9._____

2._____   10._____

3._____   (11)._____

4._____   (12)._____

5._____   (13)._____

6._____   (14)._____

7._____   (15)._____

8._____

Make a List of Your *Best* Friends

The third type of friend is your *best* friends, the three to five people who are your intimates and your close support group. This list often includes family members.

Write out a list of your best friends. Once more, don't worry if there are not five. As you continue this journey, your list will grow. Remember, your three to five today may not be your three to five next week; people drift among layers and sometimes fall out of them altogether.

1._____

2._____

3._____

(4)._____

(5)._____

Make a List of Companion(s)

Once more, don't worry if you cannot name a companion. These relationships are rare and often come along once in a lifetime. Far more than a soulmate, your companion(s) shares a connection or congruence with almost every aspect of your being. They are physically, mentally, spiritually, and emotionally compatible with you.

1._____

(2)._____

A tribe is a social group having a common character or interest comprising fans, acquaintances, friends, and companions. Let's find and embrace our tribe. Relying on, *needing* them is not a sign of weakness. It shows that you want to be the best person you can be, and you are not afraid to admit it. We all need a helping hand at times. Sometimes we are not enough on our own.

Hopefully, this step has encouraged you to take a moment and consider your tribe(s) and the impact the members have upon your life. Consider the things you value most—your essentials—and how these diverse people (both past and present) add layered nuance to who you are becoming. Healthy tribes piece together the fragments of our lives, and they complement *who we are* until what emerges is whole, meaningful, new, and better. May we continue the journey of finding healing, finding ourselves, and finding others.

Step 10

In Which We Seek To Understand Attachment Styles

One of the most life-changing ideas introduced to me during two years of therapy with my psychologist Dr. Steve was *Attachment Theory*. Understanding this relatively unknown method of relationship styles gave me the confidence to choose a new life companion that complemented me. It has helped me assess new tribe members more effectively and better understand existing tribe members. The attachment theory applies best to the friend and companion categories.

John Bowlby is the father of this research. He defined attachment as a "lasting psychological connectedness between human beings."[81] Bowlby was a British psychologist and psychoanalyst who believed that early childhood attachments played a critical role in later development and mental functioning. His work, along with the work of psychologist Mary Ainsworth, contributed to the development of attachment theory.

Bowlby believed that children are born with a biologically-programmed tendency to seek and remain close to attachment figures. This provides nurturance and comfort, and aids in the child's survival. Sticking close to a caregiver ensures that the child's needs are met and that he or she is protected from dangers in the environment.[82] This fascinating study that was initially developed in a children's hospital environment has far-reaching ramifications in our search for a new and better tribe.

Adult Attachment Styles

Attachment psychologists who study adult relationships have identified three primary styles of attachment: *secure, anxious, and avoidant*. Our adult attachment styles can be indicators of a childhood environment that continues to affect us throughout life in our close relationships. These styles refer to the level of anxiety and avoidance in a relationship and one's response to these variables.

Although beyond the scope of this book, a thorough study of how our childhood environment affects our tribal relationships will provide valuable context and help in the search for belonging. Our heart gets emotional food from nurturing parents at the most crucial time of development. Loving contact as we grow up is as vital as human nutrition. If we don't get it, the result is emotional starvation.

Children have an absolute requirement for safe, ongoing physical and emotional closeness, and we ignore this only at a high cost. Believe it or not, as late as the 1960s, primarily because of Freudian philosophy, parents were only allowed to visit their hospitalized children for one hour per week.

In the 1950s, as a psychiatrist and medical doctor, Bowlby realized the error of this practice and introduced a revolutionary idea—that the quality of the connection to loved ones is key to the development of personality and to a person's natural way of connecting with others.

This idea, this theory, has literally revolutionized developmental psychology. The attachment theory was, and perhaps still is, radically out of line with our culture's established social and psychological ideas of adulthood: that maturity means being independent and self-sufficient.

The notion of the invulnerable warrior who faces life and danger alone is long ingrained in our culture. Consider James Bond, the iconic impervious man, still going strong after four decades. In contrast, Bowlby talks about dependency, and how being able, from "the cradle to the grave" to turn to others for emotional support is a sign and source of strength.

The Codependency Myth

We need each other. Unfortunately, the idea of codependency has gained wide acceptance. This is particularly true with so-called "Christian" counselors. I have found that many of them have the theory of co-dependence ingrained, and they refuse to accept (or have never even heard of) attachment theory.

During the five years of conflict and turmoil in my marriage of thirty years, I told a Christian counselor about the lack of affection and closeness in our relationship. He said that it was wrong to depend on my mate for intimacy —he felt we had become codependent on each other. He suggested I have a love affair with God.

Ever the questioner, this prompted an inquiry that became the basis for my first book, *Sex, Lies & Religion*. It asked, "Have you ever had an experience with God that was so amazing it exceeded your wildest and most fulfilling sexual moment?" Frankly, I have not. After asking hundreds of people that question, the overwhelming majority answered no.

I would provide a personal word of caution here. Be wary of Christian counselors who advise being secure in your faith and getting emotional support from God instead of your tribe and your companion. That advice may sound spiritual, but the Attachment Theory research from Bowlby and Ainsworth disproves the codependency myth. We need to depend on people we can touch, see, smell, and feel in our daily lives for intimacy and comfort. A tribe of people we can lean on, and they, in turn, can lean on us.

Researchers and psychologists Amir Levine and Rachel Heller write, "The codependency movement and other currently popular self-help approaches portray relationships in a way that is remarkably similar to the views held in the first half of the twentieth century about the child-parent bond (i.e., the 'happy child' who is free of unnecessary attachments)."

"Today's experts offer advice that goes something like this: Your happiness is something that should come from within and should not be dependent on your lover or tribe. Your well-being is not their responsibility, and theirs is not yours. Each person needs to look after themselves. You should learn not to allow your inner peace to be disturbed by the person you are closest to."

"If your partner acts in a way that undermines your sense of security, you should be able to distance yourself from the situation emotionally, 'keep the focus on yourself,' and stay on an even keel. If you can't do that, there might be something wrong with you. You might be too enmeshed with the other person, or 'codependent,' and you must learn to set better 'boundaries.'"

They continue, "The basic premise underlying this point of view is that the ideal relationship is one between two self-sufficient people who unite in a mature, respectful way while maintaining clear boundaries. If you develop a strong dependency on your partner, you are deficient in some way and are advised to work on yourself to become more 'differentiated' (basically, differentiation means a healthy separation of one's self), and develop a 'greater sense of self.' The worst possible scenario is that you will end up needing your partner, which is equated with 'addiction' to him or her, and addiction, we all know, is a dangerous prospect."

"While the teachings of the codependency movement remain immensely helpful in dealing with family members who suffer from substance abuse (as was the initial intention), they can be misleading and even damaging when applied indiscriminately to all relationships. Many of us have been influenced by these schools of thought. But biology tells a very different story."[83]

Here are three statements that will help you determine your attachment style.

Secure

If you feel comfortable with intimacy with your friend or companion and don't obsess much about the relationship or about your tribe member's ability to love you back, but coast along with it—you're probably *secure*.

Anxious

If you crave intimacy and closeness but have a lot of insecurities about where the relationship is going, and little things your tribe member does tend to set you off— you're probably *anxious*.

Avoidant

If you feel uncomfortable when things become too close and intimate and value your independence and freedom more than the relationship, and don't tend to worry about your tribe member's feelings or commitment toward you—you're probably avoidant.

You may find it useful to learn that two dimensions primarily determine attachment styles:

1) Your comfort with intimacy and closeness (or the degree to which you try to *avoid* intimacy.)

2) Your anxiety about your tribe member's friendship and attentiveness and your preoccupation with the relationship.

Cindy Hazan and Philip Shaver, pioneers in the field of adult attachment, published a "love quiz" in the *Rocky Mountain News*.[84] In the first question of the quiz, they asked people to choose the one description out of three that best described their feelings and attitudes in relationships. The following statements characterize the three attachment styles:

1) I find it relatively easy to get close to others and am comfortable depending on them and having them rely on me. I don't often worry about being abandoned or about someone getting too close to me.

2) I am somewhat uncomfortable being close to others; I find it difficult to trust them completely, difficult to allow myself to depend on them. I am nervous when anyone gets too close, and often, love partners want me to be more intimate than I feel comfortable being.

3) I find that others are reluctant to get as close as I would like. I often worry that my partner doesn't love me or won't want to stay with me. I want to merge completely with another person, and this desire sometimes scares people away.

If you chose statement one, you probably have the *secure* attachment style. Statement two is an indicator of the *avoidant* attachment style, and statement three is a measure of the *anxious* attachment style.

A free attachment style psychological assessment tool can be found at *randyelrod.com/resources*. If you are serious about having a *better* tribe and understanding the nuances of this life-changing relationship theory, I highly recommend reading the book *Attached: The New Science of Adult Attachment and How It Can Help You Find—and Keep—Love* by Amir Levine and Rachel Heller.

In it, you will find helpful information and expanded attachment theory assessments for yourself and prospective tribe members. They explain how each style complements the others and how to choose those with whom you will be compatible. Please note that the authors have written primarily for those in a romantic relationship, but the basic principles correlate to tribal relationships such as friends and companions. The worth of the comprehensive assessments alone far exceeds the price of the book.

A Brief Overview of Attachment Theory

In attachment theory, adults show patterns of attachment to their friends and companions similar to the patterns of attachment of children with their parents. This similarity helps explain the full range of behaviors in adult relationships.

Levine and Heller explain that in a fundamental sense, *secure* people feel comfortable with intimacy and are usually warm and loving. A*nxious* people crave close affection, are often preoccupied with their relationships, and tend to worry about their partner's ability to love them back. A*voidant* people equate intimacy with a loss of independence and always try to minimize closeness.[85]

People with each of these attachment styles differ in:
- their view of togetherness
- the way they deal with conflict
- their attitude toward intimacy
- their ability to communicate their wishes and needs
- their expectations from their tribe members and the relationship

Estimates say that over 50 to 60 percent of the adult population is secure, around 15 to 20 percent are anxious, 20 to 25 percent are avoidant, and the remaining 3 to 5 percent fall into a fourth, less common disorganized category. Understanding a potential tribe member's attachment style is an easy and reliable way to understand and predict their behavior.

Levine and Heller write that "It is understood our attachment styles are influenced by a variety of factors, one of which is the way our parents cared for us, but other factors come into play, including our genes and life experiences. They believe it is possible for a person to change their attachment style and consciously work toward becoming more secure instead of letting life sway them every which way."[86]

By determining attachment styles of acquaintances who are potential friends and companions, we can better choose potential tribe members and gain more clarity in our current relationships. A tribe member's behavior will no longer seem disconcerting, but somewhat predictable under the circumstances. *"Attachment theory is based on the assertion that the need to be in a close relationship is embedded in our genes."*[87]

By understanding that people vary greatly in their need for intimacy and closeness and that these differences create conflict—attachment styles can offer us a new way of looking at tribal relationships. It is important to note that attachment theory does not label behaviors as healthy or unhealthy. None of the attachment styles is in itself seen as wrong. On the contrary, actions that were previously seen as odd or misguided can seem understandable, predictable, even expected. It can help us make informed decisions in our search for a new and better tribe.

As we take the journey to regain belonging, attachment theory says first to find the right people to depend on, and then travel down the road with them. When the tribe is unaware of and therefore unable to meet our basic attachment needs, we tend to experience a lack of belonging that leaves us more exposed to various ailments. Not only is our essential well-being sacrificed when we are in a relationship with a tribe who doesn't provide a secure base, but as we saw with the residents of Roseto, so is our physical health.

Our tribe powerfully affects our ability to thrive in the world. Not only does the group influence how we feel about ourselves but whether we will attempt to achieve our purpose and meaning in life. Having a tribe (particularly our friends and companions) that does not understand our attachment style and the essentials of our being can be a discouraging experience.

Levine and Heller teach that understanding attachment styles will change your perceptions of new people you meet, and it will give you surprising insight into your current tribal relationships. However, they caution that determining other people's attachment styles is usually more complicated than identifying your own.

Here are what the authors call the *Five Golden Rules* to help evaluate attachment style in others:

1) Determine whether the person seeks intimacy and closeness.

2) Assess how preoccupied they are with the relationship and how sensitive they are to rejection.

3) Don't rely on one "symptom," look for various signs.

4) Assess his/her reaction to effective communication.

5) Listen and look for what they are *not* saying or doing.[88]

Attachment theory helps us understand that we all have different capacities for intimacy. It is relatively easy to find new and better tribe members when they have a secure attachment style. Problems may arise if you have an anxious style and are trying to become a close friend or companion with someone who has an avoidant style, or vice-versa. Amir and Levine call this the "anxious-avoidant" trap, and they do an excellent job explaining the implications. It is difficult but not impossible to make this type of tribal relationship work.

This theory shows us that our attachment needs are valid and that we shouldn't feel guilty about depending on others. I have come to believe there is a direct correlation between a rigorous assessment of attachment styles and better tribal relationships. One of the most crucial take aways from this chapter, *and* this book is that *relationships should not be haphazard.* We must be intentional and proactive. Belonging to a cohesive tribe can be one of the most fulfilling of human experiences, far beyond other opportunities that life has to offer.

Bonus

Seventeen <u>MORE</u> Steps To A New (and Better) Tribe

1. Utilize the ZERO Principle

A friend told me this story he heard from a respected mentor. His wife was always disappointed by friends not living up to her expectations. Finally, he said, "Honey, that is the difference between you and me. You get a new friend, and you instantly expect them to be all in—to be 'besties' and all that. You want 100 percent from them but because of the demands of life they can give you only fifty percent, and you end up complaining; and when they only give you ten percent you despair." He continued, "But with my friends, I try to start out the relationship expecting nothing, and when they give me ten percent I'm grateful, and when they give me fifty percent I am ecstatic."

I call it the *Zero Principle*. Instead of approaching each relationship expecting 100 percent—but being bitterly disappointed by getting only fifty percent—let's learn to come to each relationship expecting zero and being pleasantly surprised when we receive anything at all.

As the full impact of the loss of my lifelong tribe began to set in, I thought it best to relocate to a new city for a time to clear my head. I had a few acquaintances there, and one seemed to be a prospect for friendship. We discovered many shared interests—cooking, food and wine, coffee, and the arts. In the throes of grief and loneliness, I went all-in with this new relationship.

But frustration quickly set in as it became clear that a close friendship was not possible with this person. Even though we had myriad things in common, there were many essentials we did not share. He had a young family and a growing business that demanded much of his time while I was an empty-nester and my schedule was much more flexible. The friendship never materialized.

My partner (now wife) gently reminded me of the Zero Principle. She said it seemed that I was expecting 100 percent from this relationship. As I spent time reflecting on her wisdom, I knew she was right, and I determined to be grateful for the ten to twenty percent I was receiving from this person. It was hard to admit that this charismatic and fun individual was not destined to be a close friend and share an intimate relationship. Instead, he would make a high-quality acquaintance, and we could continue to enjoy our casual and sporadic times of cooking and music without any undue expectations on my part.

When the messy reality of life happens, it is easy to forget basic guidelines. This is one to remember. Instead of approaching each relationship expecting 100 percent—but being bitterly disappointed by getting less—it is better to come to each relationship expecting zero and being pleasantly surprised when we receive anything at all.

2. Know The Difference Between Honesty and Vulnerability

Honesty means *freedom* from deceit or fraud. Vulnerability means being *susceptible* to woundedness or hurt. The words in italics (freedom and susceptible) help delineate two words (honesty and vulnerability) that are often used synonymously.

How can we go in the direction of full honesty and still be protected within the buffer surrounding our vulnerability? Honesty refers to the quality of being upfront and forthright. Vulnerability refers to something more emotional and exposes fragile aspects of one's soul. To be honest means we're not attempting to hide anything. To be vulnerable means there's risk involved, it is an expression of trust that leaves open the possibility of hurt.

Recognizing the difference between someone extending honesty or vulnerability determines what response is appropriate. In my experience, people looking for a new and better tribe often have trouble knowing whether to be honest or vulnerable, and I believe this leads them to interact in unintentionally problematic ways.

When you demonstrate honesty, it's a way to express a reality about yourself, like your favorite artist or birthplace. Honesty doesn't necessarily leave the door open for further questions. But when you demonstrate vulnerability, it invites the other into closer intimacy, you are lowering your defenses and signaling a desire to connect more deeply.

Vulnerability allows a trustworthy friend to speak words of love and compassion into tender places, and it often results in a reciprocated openness. But when vulnerability is shown to an acquaintance whose trust has not been earned, it can result in deep wounds and severe scars, and it makes future transparency difficult or impossible. Unlike honesty, vulnerability requests interaction from the person who receives it. Another inappropriate response to this exposure of self would be withdrawing or retreating, leaving the other person susceptible without respecting the weight of what they've revealed.

When people lose belonging and begin to reconnect with a new tribe, I think it's inevitable that initial friendship conversations will involve vulnerability. We're still exploring our own essentials and discovering how other people are going to react to us, and the dialogue in those moments matters because we're opening these tender places for perhaps the first time.

As we find healing, we'll reach a certain level of confidence and comfort in our selves, and understand the difference between *acknowledging* our physical and mental processes to prospective friends for the sake of honesty, and gradually *revealing* our more intimate spiritual and emotional aspects in order to build a foundation of true friendship and vulnerability. We must be careful not to share the essentials of our spirit (heart) or our soul to those who have not earned the right to care for them.

3. Seasons of Relationship

One of the few passages of the *Hebrew Bible* that still speak to me is the third chapter of the book of *Ecclesiastes*. My paraphrase of verses 1-8 says:

There is a season for everything,
a time to be born and a time to die,
a time to search and a time to count your losses,
a time to hold on and a time to let go,
a time to embrace and a time to part,

a time to build and a time to deconstruct,
a time to do and a time to be,
a time for others and a time for me,
a time to grieve and a time to heal,
a time to weep and a time to laugh,
a time to mourn and a time to dance,
a time to be silent and a time to speak,
a time to love and a time to hate,
a time for conflict and a time for peace,
a time to make love and a time to abstain,
a time to friend and a time to unfriend,
there is a season for everything.

Relationships change, and not always for the best. We may discover that a friend with whom we have had a long and vital relationship is no longer someone we enjoy being around. Perhaps you have changed and become someone different, and what bound the relationship together no longer exists.

We can hold someone dear in the present moment, honoring the deep place they occupy in our life history—but know the season of friendship may have ended. When we honestly evaluate a past relationship we can be genuinely grateful for its beauty. But trying to force a friendship past its season is a disservice to both parties.

We are always in process, and we continually change throughout life. There are relationships for different places and different times, and they need to be congruent with who we are. But if you're not spending a lot of time together and don't have much in common anymore, it is okay to let that friendship go. Sending a Christmas card may be enough.

4. Steer Away From Toxic People

T he word toxic comes from the Latin phrase *toxikon*, which means "arrow poison," points out Theo Veldsman, head of Industrial Psychology and People Management at the University of Johannesburg. "In a literal sense, the term means to kill (or poison) in a targeted way."[89] I call toxic people vampires because they suck the life out of you.

Tribal relationships should be two-way streets that involve mutual care throughout the journey. We thrive on companionship and entering into a toxic relationship can result in severe inner conflict. How do we steer away from bad relationships? How do we repair them?

Kristen Fuller, MD, provides valuable questions and insight when dealing with a toxic relationship.[90]

How does the person treat others?

Look at how the person treats the people closest to them. Do they speak poorly about family members, or display signs of aggression toward parents, friends or co-workers? Is the person in constant conflict with other people? The best decision may be to walk away if the person is unwilling to change.

How does the person deal with conflict?

Does the person refuse to address issues or apologize for their actions? If this person acts spitefully after the conflict and spreads rumors—that is a major red flag. A person who truly cares for you will attempt to make amends. You can learn a lot about someone's character by observing how they deal with conflict.

How does the person make you feel when you are together?

Does this person talk about themselves the whole time? Do they verbally put down others? Do they constantly gossip? Take a moment to reflect on the time you spend with this person to determine how you feel after each experience. If you feel drained and not energized when you spend time together, you may need to take a step back from this person to protect yourself. This is not selfish, but an act of self-love.

What are the person's past experiences with relationships?

History repeats itself. Although people do grow and mature, their past experiences truly shape them. Does this person have close long-term friends? Or do they sever relationships quickly? What happened with the person's past relationships? It is vital that you are aware of past behavior to determine if they have taken proper steps to make positive changes.

Does this person make you feel important?

Do they demean you in front of others? Do they tend to hurt you when you are down? Does the person trivialize things that are important to you? Do they ignore your requests and needs? If you are having more bad moments than good moments, you may need to steer away.

Important note: Many people who were raised in toxic environments find it difficult to identify healthy relationships because they're not familiar with them. It is usually easier for others to see the toxicity. Even though it may be hard to accept, listen to those you trust.

Dr. Fuller states, "One of the most difficult therapeutic problems I see is helping patients who have been preyed upon, or 'toxified,' to accept a kind and loving experience without fleeing. They are attracted to what is familiar— more toxic relationships, which they often experience as normal. It may be scary for them to cut these ties. It's sad, but true, that they may even believe what the toxic person says about them—that they're stupid, ugly, worthless, or whatever."

Acknowledging that you are in a toxic relationship may be hard, as you recover from the loss of your former tribe. When we are lonely, we tend to be blinded by temporary happiness. Even though we know the relationship is damaging, our emotions can exert undue influence over rational decisions. But these honest questions can help us rid ourselves of toxic people as we continue the quest for a new and better tribe.

5. Six Types of People You Should Never Be Friends With

I f you share your friendship with the wrong person, they can quickly become one more piece of flying debris in your loss of belonging. We need stable connections in situations like these—something akin to a sturdy tree firmly planted in the ground. In a television interview, Brené Brown tells Oprah Winfrey[91] that we definitely want to *avoid* the following relationships.

1) The friend who actually feels shame for you and gasps and confirms how horrified you should be.

You have just told your friend a hardship you experienced. She gives you a shoulder to cry on. There's an awkward pause. Next moment the situation flips, and it's your duty to comfort her and elevate her mood. If you have been in this scenario, then it's highly recommended to stay away from this person. These are the type of people who will hear you out and talk to you about your feelings for the first few minutes. In no time, suddenly, the whole focus shifts to their problems and you are discussing their issues. This just proves how unimportant your feelings are to that person.

2) The friend who confuses connection with the opportunity to one-up you.

("Well, that's nothing. Listen what happened to me...")

If the majority of your friend's sentences starts with: "oh, but you don't know what happened to me…" then you have a mistake to rectify. When you turn your head towards your friend for comfort in a situation, you expect them to boost your morale. Instead, they try putting you down by telling you how they faced a much worse situation. Go ahead and give them the bragging rights and then you should immediately walk away from such friends.

3) The friend who is all about making it better and out of her own discomfort refuses to acknowledge that you can actually make terrible choices.

("You're exaggerating. It wasn't that bad.")

Often there are times when you share a story with your friend, and they try their best to cheer you up. Yet they end up doing something foolish, such as denying the fact that the events in the story actually happened or say it's an exaggerated version. From their perspective, they are trying to put you in a spot where something so embarrassing or bad couldn't happen to you because of the "perfection" you possess, but it actually means that they aren't acknowledging the truth. "Nah! I don't believe this could happen to you. You are smart enough to tackle it. You are awesome. I bet its nothing." Having such friends who express their opinion by making you look god-like should strictly be avoided.

4) The friend who is so uncomfortable with vulnerability that she scolds you.

("How did you let this happen?")

We all have come across that one friend who consistently has to find a person or a reason to blame for any action or emotional vulnerability. Instead of assigning personal responsibility, they try to pass it on to someone else. "Who did this to you? Who was that person? How could such a tragedy happen to you? What were you thinking about?"

Instead of acknowledging the ability to take personal responsibility, they try to pin it down on others. This would always make you believe that you weren't at fault and slowly you could develop this habit of finding other people to blame. Avoid a friend that is uncomfortable with vulnerability.

5) The friend who needs you to be the pillar of worthiness and authenticity, who can't help you because she's too disappointed in your imperfections.

This type of friend will always look up to you. They consider you to be the benchmark and you are their role models when it comes to certain situations. To some extent, this is a positive approach, yet once they experience disappoint due to your flaws, it becomes a burden to live up their expectations. These type of people would pull you down by setting unreasonably high expectations. Failing to meet them means anxiety and constant reminders of how you disappoint them.

6) The friend who responds with sympathy (*"I feel so sorry for you."*) rather than empathy (*"I get it, I feel with you, and I've been there."*)

These people regularly respond to a difficult situation with, "oh I feel so bad for you, or everything is fine," or a "God bless you." They sympathize, yet they fail to recognize your pain and express their empathy. Instead of trying to fit in your shoes to actually experience what you did, they say things like "I feel sorry for you." This shows inadequacy in understanding what you actually felt.

6. Identify Common Essentials

You ou previously made a list of your top four physical, mental, spiritual, and emotional essentials in Step 6, item #2. It stands to reason, the more commonalities you have with someone, the more likely you are to progress in a relationship. As you look for a new and better tribe, pay attention when your essentials repeatedly show up in others.

Having one or more of your four physical essentials similar or in common with someone may indicate a prospective fan.

If they have one or more of the mental essentials it may suggest a possible new acquaintance. Furthermore, if they have one or more of the spiritual essentials similar or in common, it may indicate a prospective friend. When on the rarest of occasions they also share several of the emotional essentials it may suggest a potential companion.

It is important to note that context is critical here. It is not unusual to find someone who has a commonality with any one of your essentials. But when the totals begin to add up, chances are excellent they are a prospective new tribe member. This does not mean you will be tribal twins. There may be differences which can enhance the relationship. We will see this more in the next step as we talk about *homophily* (love of the same). But when the common essentials begin to add up—a healthy, productive friendship could be in the making.

Copy your top four physical, mental, spiritual, and emotional essentials from Step 6, List #2 and look for them in your search for a new and better tribe.

Physical/Body—Prospective Fan

1._____
2._____
3._____
4._____

Mental/Mind—Prospective Acquaintance

5._____

6._____

7._____

8._____

Spiritual/Spirit—Prospective Friend

9._____

10._____

11._____

12._____

Emotional/Soul—Prospective Companion

13._____

14._____

15._____

16._____

7. Resist Homophily

I n the 1950s, sociologists coined the term *homophily* to explain our tendency to link up with one another in ways that confirm instead of testing our core beliefs. The name didn't catch on, but the concept is now enjoying a renaissance, in part because it has been repeatedly invoked to explain America's divisive political atmosphere.

"Similarity breeds connection," sociologists Miller McPherson, Lynn Smith-Lovin, and James Cook wrote, "and the result is that people's personal networks are homogeneous."[92]

While it is vital to identify common essentials as we find a new and better tribe, we need fans, acquaintances, and friends who will give us alternative perspectives. Chances are our former tribe was homogenous, and while similar people make us feel comfortable, we need to look for a few tribe members who are different as well. Having friends with the same essentials but different opinions is possible. So how do we get opposites back into the equation?

David Burkus in his book *Friend of A Friend* suggests doing an audit of your connections. Our social networks provide an easy way to do this. Look at some of the people with whom you have interacted the most over the past months on *Facebook* or *LinkedIn*. Look at what groups they "like." You may be tempted to unfriend some of them but don't. If their connections are different from you, you probably need them in your life more than you think.

While common essentials are crucial in establishing new close friendships, people with different beliefs bring diversity and a viewpoint that can prove beneficial to our world-view. Several of my old (and new) acquaintances and friends have different political and religious views, yet they are not adversarial. They add contrasting values and opinions to life that resist the monochromatic hues of homophily. A more diverse tribe adds color to the mosaic of our lives.

8. Develop Charisma

We tend to think charisma is an innate gift. After all, you can't teach someone to be Barack Obama. But a *Harvard Review* article states "it's a learnable skill or, rather, a set of skills that have been practiced since antiquity."[93]

Why is it that some people seem to exude charisma or presence which captivates and influences those around them, while others have the opposite effect? Can charisma be learned and developed? The answer is a most definite yes. However, it cannot be faked. *Charisma is the ability to help people feel intimate in a non-intimate space.*

First, we need to understand presence. Presence is defined as the ability to project a sense of ease, confidence, and self-assurance. It accompanies all charismatic people. They are "comfortable in their own skin." Researchers have observed that those with an infectious personality unintentionally cause others to copy their body language and facial expressions.

Police officers and our military are taught "command presence." Command presence is essentially presenting yourself as someone in authority—trusted and respected. This is partially done by how you look, how you carry yourself, how you act, and how you speak. But genuine charisma does away with having to be authoritative. You merely have to offer people the gift of your presence.

Second, we need to understand the difference between large-group and small-group charisma. Many people who have large-group charisma have no small-group charm whatsoever. They are not comfortable with small groups, and they gravitate to one person or one corner of the room. However, when you are in the presence of a small-group charismatic person, you always feel as if you were better having been in their presence than before the encounter. You almost always leave with something of value. It may be merely the gift of their presence, their attention, their listening, or their concern—but you always feel richer.

Three Ways to Practice Charisma

1) Pay Attention to Your Emotional State
Charisma is, in part, the result of controlling which emotional state you go into. Practice being genuinely optimistic and genuinely curious.

2) Focus
The only way you can be charismatic is by paying attention to other people. When you are with other people, what are you focusing on? Are you thinking about what you will say to them? If so, you're blocking your charisma. Don't focus inward, instead pay attention to the person in front of you.

3) Listen
Simply because we have ears and can hear doesn't mean we know how to listen. How do you listen to others? Do you listen to be able to one-up the story? Do you pay attention to learn about that person's connections? Do you listen to learn how you can impress that person with your knowledge? When you hear others in that way, you damage your chance to be charismatic because you look selfish.

Instead, listen with affection and empathy. Assume you genuinely like that person. Listen as though you sincerely care what happens in that person's life. Listen to hear, not to fix or solve. The critical ingredient to charisma is being present to others.[94]

9. Questions Instead of Answers

H ave you noticed people who are not self-aware rarely ask questions? And if they do, they don't listen to the answer. Self-awareness is an important trait in finding a new and better tribe. We are all born with a natural curiosity and the ability to question. The average 4-year-old asks their parents hundreds of questions a day. By the time we are adults, we manage to pose only a few in a given day.

Asking questions helps get to know someone new without talking about what you do and the weather. In these divisive times, it's probably best to avoid talking about politics, religion, and sexual orientation at the outset of a new relationship. One way to get to know someone is to learn what they do in their spare time and about their preferences.

Below are a few sample questions from *Lifehack*[95] to ask when getting to know a prospective tribe member. I have paraphrased a few of them.

Start by asking, "Would you rather..."

— Watch *Game of Thrones*, *House of Cards* or *This Is Us*? (Use and compare shows you find most relevant.)

— Go to a movie or a ballgame?

— Have a cocktail, a glass of wine or craft beer?

— Vacation in the Caribbean or Alaska, and why?

— Stay in a hotel or an Airbnb?

— Hike, bike, swim, or run?

— Have a night out or evening in?

— Watch TV or read a book?

— Use Facebook, Instagram or Twitter?

It is helpful to get to know someone by learning how they think. Here are a few sample questions to get you started.

— If the sky was the limit and you could do anything you want right now, what would it be?

— What destination is on your travel bucket list?

— Where is the favorite place you have been in your travels?

— Who is your favorite author?

— What is your favorite book? Why?

— Who do you look up to and why?

— What does your perfect day look like?

— What is one thing that you can't live without right now?

— What is the one thing that should be taught in school that isn't already?

— If you were to create a piece of art, what would the subject be?

— What one thing would you change if you had to do it over?

— If you could go back in time, what year would you travel to?

— How would your friends describe you?

Instead of asking a straightforward question, qualify it by saying: "Sports are fun, but I find movies to be a richer experience. I recently saw _____ and loved it. What do you prefer, a ballgame or a movie?"

Don't pepper them with one question after another; give a query time to lead into a conversation naturally. Once the person tells you their preference between a ballgame or a movie, ask why.

One of my favorite questions to ask a new acquaintance over a leisurely dinner is by Krista Tippet, a PBS host and author of the best-selling book, *Becoming Wise: An Inquiry into the Mystery and Art of Living*. Tippet suggests the following question: "What was the spiritual background to your childhood?" She feels it encourages people to speak more openly from the story of their life—about what they believe and who they are.

To paraphrase the author Margaret Atwood, "The answers you get from others depend on the questions you pose." Asking the right questions is a crucial step in finding a new and better tribe.

10. Ulterior Motives

F ans have ulterior motives. Prospective tribe members should not. One of my pet peeves is someone asking for an appointment under the guise of a desire to know me better, and after a few obviously canned questions, begins a pitch to sell me insurance or have me join a multi-level marketing platform such as *Amway* or as it is now called *Quixtar*. Another irritation is when someone wants to "befriend" me exclusively for my connections, influence, or ideas.

When searching for a new and better tribe, abandon the ulterior motives at the door. Always focus on creating friendships first, and develop business deals later. I never seek out relationships with people on a business level. That's lame if you ask me. This is a mistake made by many. They reach out to someone and instantly think about how that person can benefit them professionally or in their business.

11. Pay Attention

Our relationships are more satisfying if we pay attention to one another. Rick Hanson says in his book *Buddha's Brain: The Practical Neuroscience of Happiness, Love and Wisdom*, "'attention shapes the brain.' What we pay attention to is what we will build in our brain tissue."[96] Be purposeful in your search for tribe members (particularly those with whom you work, play, and live) be pro-active, have eagle eyes for similarities and patterns.

Attention is noticing and being with someone without trying to change the focus. It takes the time to explore fully, to discover whatever there is to know about something, to watch as things change by themselves without our trying to "fix" anything. Attention is patient, and attention is kind. It protects and trusts and does not pass judgment. No rush. No burden. No criticism.

Walking through life in this way requires an attention to the present that is extremely difficult to maintain. In his book *Wilderness Essays,* John Muir, the famous naturalist, author, and environmental philosopher recounts this prescient observation about one of his many trips of exploration in the American West. "As we sat by the camp-fire the brightness of the sky brought on a long talk with the Indians about the stars; and their eager, childlike attention was refreshing to see as compared with the decent, deathlike apathy of weary civilized people, in whom natural curiosity has been quenched in toil and care, and poor, shallow comfort."[97]

Walking can be a profoundly spiritual exercise in paying attention. An activity that has greatly helped me is walking meditation. It is simple to do. Go to the woods or a country path. Begin to stroll slowly. Then simply be aware. Take one breath for each step. One breath, one step.

It is about awareness—paying attention. The *Kabbalists* (Kabbalah is a form of Jewish mysticism) teach it is about taking an everyday activity—in this case walking—and raising it, elevating it from the physical realm to the divine.

It is about making Heaven manifest on earth. It is about doing spiritual work, one step at a time.

The first time I tried this, it was a profound experience. When I finished, I immediately journaled my thoughts and feelings during the walk. The result was ten handwritten pages back and front. It was a familiar walk on a trail at our farm that I had taken countless days, but this time it had come alive. For a moment, I was like the Indians that Muir encountered. I experienced "eager, childlike attention" to the world.

We can walk our path with others in much the same way. As you have interactions with others, walk quietly and slowly with them. Then simply be aware. Take one breath for each thought. One deep breath, one idea. Life with others is about awareness and paying attention as we continue the quest for a new and better tribe.

12. Life Giving or Draining?

Here is a simple test my life coach taught me. When you are with someone, and when you finish the meeting, do a simple evaluation—did time with that person drain you or energize you? The test for me is in my shoulders where I carry stress. Are they tense or tired?

Ask yourself, did you work too much during that conversation or was it an equal give and take? We all will have unavoidable encounters that drain us, the key is to regulate and balance them with energizing appointments. Purposefully seek out tribe members in all categories (fans, acquaintances, friends, and companions) who are life-giving not life draining.

13. The Lost Art of Listening

W ho listens to you? Who pays attention? Who strains to hear your soul whispers? Listening is another attribute that endears people to each other and helps in forming a new and better tribe. The following thoughts are from my synopsis of a valuable book by Dr. Michael Nichols, *The Lost Art of Listening*. [98]

Being listened to means we are taken seriously, that our ideas and feelings are known, and ultimately it means that what we have to say matters.

The essence of good listening is empathy, which can be achieved only by suspending our preoccupation with ourselves and entering into the experience of the other person. Part intuition and part effort, it's the stuff of human connection.

Listening is such an essential part of our lives that we take it for granted. Unfortunately, most of us think of ourselves as better listeners than we are. Even infants need listening to thrive. The listened-to child grows up relatively secure and whole. The unlistened-to child lacks the understanding that forms self-acceptance and is "bent out of shape" by the wishes and anxieties of others. The need to be understood is second only to the need for food and shelter.

Parents who listen make their children feel worthwhile and appreciated. Being listened to helps build a robust and secure self, endowing the child with sufficient self-respect to develop their own unique talents and ideas and to approach relationships with confidence and tolerance.

Real listening means suspending memory, desire, and judgment—and, for a few moments at least, existing for the other person.

Genuine Listening

When listening is authentic, the emphasis is on the speaker, not the listener. An empathic response is restrained, mostly silent; following, not leading, it encourages the speaker to go deeper into his or her experience.

Counterfeit Listening

"That reminds me of the time…" (Translation: "I can top that.")

"Oh, how awful!" (Translation: "You poor, helpless thing. Here's another fine mess you got yourself into.")

"Well, if I were you…" (Translation: "Stop bothering me with your whining and do something about it.")

"Have you heard the one about…?" (Translation: "Never mind what you were saying; your concerns are boring.")

"Don't feel that way" (Translation: Don't upset me with your upset.")

Sensitive Listening

Pay attention to what the other person is saying.
Acknowledge the other person's feelings.
Listen without giving an opinion.
Listen without offering advice.
Listen without immediately agreeing or disagreeing.
Notice how the person appears to be feeling—and ask.
Ask about their day, both before and after.
Respect the person's need for quiet times.
Respect the person's need to address problems.
Listen to but don't push too hard for feelings.

Listening is a skill, and like any skill, it can be practiced and improved, but even more, it is the natural outgrowth of an attitude; an attitude of caring and concern for other people. These attitudes when practiced reciprocally are the building blocks of a powerful tribe. Listening isn't a need we have; it's a gift we give.

14. Don't Throw All Former Tribe Members Out With The Bath Water

S ome former tribe members are more valuable than you might think. There's incredible power lying dormant in your past relationships. Old tribe members (with whom you have fallen out of contact) often have new ways of thinking that may be surprisingly similar to your present mindset. Connecting with old fans, acquaintances, or friends may provide connections with potential "new" tribe members.

For example, a casual acquaintance from ten years previous contacted me to do *48 Hours of Solitude* (a guided experience I lead that I had mentioned a few weeks past on social networks). At that time, he lived in the Tampa Bay area, and I was in Austin, Texas. We worked out the details, and he traveled to Austin for the event.

That decision led to this person from my past tribe (whom I previously knew little about) gradually becoming a friend. I had wrongly assumed that he still had the same worldview that I had abandoned, but to my surprise, our values had grown more congruent. Our relationship has resulted in natural connections with his friends. They have now become new and better tribe members for me.

Another bonus is our history. That friend and I share stories from a decade ago that bring a rich context to our present lives. The majority of my friends know nothing about my past, and I treasure that. But there is something about having a few people in your life who can cry and laugh with you about times gone by.

Alumni networks, trade organizations, professional groups, *LinkedIn*, and *Facebook* groups are ideal places to reconnect with old tribe members and to get a feel for the larger tribe within your access. If you can't find a group, start your own.

15. Skip Mixers—Share Activities Instead

David Burkus in his book *Friend of A Friend*[99] believes we should bypass networking events. He says they are not helpful and will probably not lead us to new tribe members. The author cites research that suggests we are better off engaging in activities that draw a cross-section of people and letting natural connections with others form as we participate in tasks together. He believes working together brings people together.

His research suggests that our time is better spent seeking out activities with a shared purpose that evokes passion or emotion, requires interdependence, and has something at stake. These shared activities draw a more diverse group of people and create stronger bonds among participants.

Here are a few shared activity suggestions to get your thinking started:

—Community Service Programs such as *Habitat for Humanity*

—Recreational sports leagues, yoga, martial arts, or hobby clubs

—Nonprofit boards or committees

—Professional associations such as Chamber of Commerce, PTA, or merchants associations

— At-work special projects teams

16. Influencers Dinner

"The fundamental element that defines the quality of our lives is the people we surround ourselves with and the conversations we have with them." Inspired by this idea, Jon Levy dedicated himself to understanding what causes people in our culture to connect.

In 2009 he created *The Influencers Dinner*, a private community and secret dining experience with the mission of bringing influential people together. The hope was that by bringing thought leaders and tastemakers together, it would improve the quality of their lives, their communities, and hopefully one day the world.

It all begins when twelve influencers from various industries attend each dinner.

The *Influencers Dinner* is known for being highly structured:

- The guest list is kept secret.

- Guests do not know one another beforehand.

- Guests are asked not to discuss their work or achievements.

- All attendees help prepare a simple meal where no cooking experience is necessary.

- Once seated at the dinner table, all attendees take turns guessing the professions of each fellow guest.

For more information: http://www.jonlevytlb.com/influencers

17. Celebrate Birthdays

A birthday is a landmark which evokes memories and these moments of nostalgia can be positive or negative. A wide range of emotions is attached to this day. Knowing this, throughout my life, I have tried to send birthday acknowledgments to my tribe members. Cy Harris, a boyhood friend of mine, believes this so strongly that for decades he has called his tribe first thing on their birthday morning and sings the *Birthday Song* to them. That annual call or voice message has become a joyous rite of passage for me for over twenty years.

If you are on the social media platform *Facebook*, by merely clicking **Home,** then **Events,** then **Birthdays,** you will see a list of your "Facebook friends," birthdays. This provides an easy and fast way to send a birthday greeting to those who are your fans, acquaintances, and friends. I try to do this every day. It takes less than five minutes.

Their profile photo allows me to put a face to a tribe member—this is particularly helpful for those who are fans and casual acquaintances. It provides a "personal" point of contact with my *Facebook* tribe at least once a year. I do my best to respond with a "like" if they comment on my birthday wish. This has moved a few people who were only fans into the acquaintance category and has helped me reconnect with people who have been unintentionally out of touch.

A happy thought on a birthday seems to carry more weight than on a regular day. Most people appreciate the time you have allocated to convey personal wishes to them. My message for 2019 is *Happy, healthy, exceptional, rocking birthday to you my Facebook friend!* I choose a different greeting each year.

Afterword

T hanks for joining me on this hope-filled quest. As I said at the beginning, there are more than a few steps to anything in this messy reality called life. But my objective is that the previous pages provide a basic map to finding healing, finding you, and finding others—a new (and better) tribe.

Above all, be faithful and attentive to your center, your essentials, and the layers of your being. This book has taught that we must work through the grief and betrayal of the loss of belonging. In some cases, we can do this more effectively by seeing a qualified, experienced, and empathic therapist. It has shown that being who we are is far more crucial than what we do, that we must seek to understand a sense of self and identify our essentials by creating a personal and ever-changing mandala.

We have sought to understand tribal relationships and the importance of experiencing a sense of place. We then applied four categories to tribal relations and utilized the insights of attachment theory. Ten steps to a new and better tribe.

All of us have a deep longing for physical, mental, spiritual, and emotional connection. Each of us innately has a fundamental need for someone to depend on. Healthy tribal relationships make us feel more secure with our self and give us comfort. They provide us with hope. A hope of belonging.

The people of the award-winning Pixar Studios are a tight-knit group of long-term collaborators who stick together and learn from one another. They are the essence of a tribe. The leaders have created a training program for their tribe members called Pixar University. On their university crest is the Latin phrase *Alienus Non Diutius* which translates means: Alone No Longer.

That phrase sums up this book. The three words express a hope-filled motto for people who dare to believe the only real fear in life is that of dying having never lived. It is for those of us who want to know our destiny and desire to become who we are meant to be. And it is for those who dare to seek a renewed sense of belonging and the joy of a new and better tribe.

There is hope. Alone No Longer.

Bonus II

An Excerpt from
A Renaissance Redneck
In A Mega-Church Pulpit
by Randy Elrod

The move back to the country was not a good one for me. The county schools were years behind the city school systems. For the first time in my life, I was at the same school for four years straight, and one would think that would provide much-needed academic stability, but I cannot remember learning one thing in high school that contributed to my future studies.

The motivation to excel in junior high quickly became apathy and disgust at teachers who were poorly trained, if at all. To make things interesting, I took bets from fellow students at the beginning of the school year that I could sleep every day in class and still make an A in the course.

The sad truth is that I won every bet and not one teacher ever woke me from my lethargy. Two things salvaged my high school years: my dad's old trombone—and believe it or not—a haircut. But let's talk about the trombone first.

Dad wouldn't allow my brother Terry and I to play football. He was afraid we would get hurt, so the only alternative for any sort of extracurricular activity was band. The band director's name was Doug Batson. He was a short man with a slender frame, frizzy golden-brown hair, and a beard with a little goatee that protruded forward, much like his pot belly. He would wear striped bell-bottom slacks with a distinct pleat and some sort of booty shoes that curled up on the ends like an elf. In fact, if he had not been such a hairy creature and a chain smoker, he could have passed for a leprechaun.

Mr. Batson was earthy and I couldn't get enough of his uninhibited self. So in tenth grade, I immediately applied to be his fourth-period "band aid." I had never met a man like him. His voice was raspy from all the cigarettes and his breathing labored, but that did not stop him from rattling off the most colorful language I had ever heard. He was the first person I ever heard drop the "f" bomb. We nerds would gather in his office at every opportunity and he would regale us with stories of wine, women, and song.

To my utter shock, one day as a few of us boys who were ulcerating to be men gathered around his office, he leaned back in his office chair and propped his pointy boots on his desk, eyes closed and arms lazily crossed behind his head. He then proceeded to fantasize aloud in vivid detail about how groovy and luscious it would be if the curvaceous blonde twin sisters who were our band majorettes would one day shed their clothes and grace the pages of *Playboy*. You could literally feel the heat increase in that cluttered office.

Later that hot spring day, during my customary nap on a school desk, consciousness wrestling with reason, I wondered if being pure really meant being happy. I remember reading in Ray Bradbury's *Something Wicked This Way Comes* that "being good is a fearful occupation; men strain at it and sometimes break in two." As my face lay against that sticky laminate desk top, fever prickled my cheeks, perspiration trickled down my legs, and I conjured beautiful (but sinful, oh how sinful) images of the twins who sat only a few seats away.

Young boys *do* love sin. Never doubt it, oh how they love it, in all shapes, sizes, colors, and smells. So when a boy's religion labels everything fun and beautiful as sin, it makes for big trouble come blossoming time. Sooner or later, natural God-given desire and passion are gonna sprout and bloom. And after considerable wrestling, I think it's far better to germinate those wildflowers at a young age rather than later in life when things are grown-up and complicated.

Doug Batson not only gave me food for my fantasies, but more importantly, he gave me visions for a future. The only thing he loved more than sin was music. And his passion for tunes was contagious. He scheduled field trips and I eagerly signed up for every one. I was working on weekends and finally had some money of my own, so I secretly ponied up for what were to be life-changing experiences.

He took us to see jazz greats Woody Herman and the Thundering Herd, Maynard Ferguson, and Bill Watrous, as well as new rock bands such as Blood, Sweat and Tears, Chicago, and the Doobie Brothers. I was mesmerized. These people made money—real money—being musicians and doing what they loved.

I couldn't understand how the church and my dad could call this captivating music "sinful." Heck, now that I think about it, everything Mr. Batson taught me was condemned as evil. Mine was not to reason why; I just knew my consciousness loved every satanic beat. I was sick and tired of being good and unhappy so I made up my mind that year to become a professional musician.

Which then brings us to the haircut.

Around that same time, as fate would have it, I met Brad Outz. He was a charismatic eleventh grader who lived next door in our latest neighborhood. Even though I went to the same high school for four years, we still moved three times. When we first moved back to the country from Chattanooga, all five of us lived in a tiny mobile home. Mom hated it, so we then temporarily moved to a rental property until Dad managed to save enough to buy a home.

Brad was a tall, slender, good-looking guy with straight natural blonde hair that hung to his shoulders and would swing as he walked. He always sported a ready smile and won my brother Terry and I as friends almost immediately.

To say he was different than any boy I had met while growing up in the mountains was an understatement. He played guitar (a beautiful yellow Fender Classic Telecaster), he drove a hip VW Beetle, religiously practiced Kung Fu, and was already honing his skills in what was to become his lifelong career as a hairstylist. Brad did not *cut* hair—he styled hair.

On a fateful autumn day in eleventh grade, with a few strokes of his scissors, Brad changed my life forever. I had been transformed, as if by magic. Turning sixteen and owning a car gave me a taste of freedom and independence so, despite Dad's protests, I had already tried to grow my hair out. But one side was much longer than the other and just stuck out in a random manner. My unruly curls and cowlick didn't help matters; combined with a stubborn case of acne, I felt and looked like an awkward, ugly loser.

Brad wet my hair, held a few strands up between his fingers, and clipped them all the same length with his scissors as we listened to Gladys Knight and the Pips sing

Best Thing That Ever Happened to Me. To his credit and my immense relief, he never picked up those damn clippers except to make sure my sideburns were even. Brad instructed me to wash my hair again, shake it, and let it dry naturally. He admonished me to never touch a comb again. The entire process took about fifteen minutes.

The next day at school, angels sang. A twelfth-grade goddess named Susan, who one day previous had not been aware of my earthly existence, asked if I could give her a ride home. As she slid in the car, all legs and flesh, a smell of summer, sweet as clover, honey-grass, and wild mint filled the car. The white cloth of her tiny lacy bloomers peeked from beneath her miniskirt as she crossed her legs.

I felt waves of dizziness as I grasped for my keys, and when I tried to say something, my tongue felt thick and useless. She was the first female other than my sister to grace the confines of my purple 1962 Pontiac Tempest Station Wagon. She would not be the last.

I quickly raced to make up for lost time. This late bloomer had not realized the sensual vacuum deep within —the voluptuous hollow, the prolonged emptiness which undulated from tip to toe—had been waiting to be filled with summer flesh. Studies were forgotten and all that mattered was quality time with the opposite sex that at long last recognized my existence.

The soothing music of Gladys Knight was soon replaced by the angst of David Bowie. My nerdy purple Pontiac station wagon was replaced by a sexy dark-green

Buick 454 four barrel. Pretty girls, loud music, and fast cars created a rush of youthful passion that sated my lack of academic fulfillment.

To read more, order Randy Elrod's fun-filled and captivating memoir:

A Renaissance Redneck In A Mega-Church Pulpit.

Book Hashtags

#TheLossOfBelonging
#ABetterTribe

Acknowledgments

Thanks to David Ballard (@okjedi) at **3 Arrows Digital** (@3arrowsdigital) for the perfect book cover design.

My sincere gratitude goes to beta-readers, John Chancellor, Beth Engleman, and Jimbo Gulley for setting aside precious time to carefully read the rough draft of this book and offer invaluable feedback.

And to my companion and wife Gina for her patience and continued encouragement for this book and for listening and enduring endless iterations over the past years.

About the Author

Randy Elrod is CEO of Creative Community, Inc, and founder of Kalien Retreat—a 54-acre oasis of solitude and refreshment in the Appalachian foothills. He enjoys time at his country home in the mountains near Nashville, TN and his cottage near the beach in Florida.

Website: randyelrod.com
All Social Networks: @randyelrod

Credits

[1] https://www.patheos.com/blogs/formerlyfundie/christian-ghosting-destructive-christian-practice-dont-talk

[2] https://archive.vcu.edu/english/engweb/transcendentalism/authors/emerson/essays/compensation.html

[3] https://www.rottentomatoes.com/m/shawshank_redemption/quotes

[4] Hebrew Bible, Matthew 22:35-40 (NIV)

[5] https://dailypoetry.me/rilke/so-we-live

[6] https://www.brainyquote.com/quotes/alfred_lord_tennyson_153702

[7] HELPGUIDE.ORG Coping with Grief and Loss. https://www.michigan.gov/documents/mdcs/griefloss.htm_617933_7.pdf

[8] Ibid

[9] Emotional Survival of First Responders. http://www.washingtonfirechiefs.com/Resources/JobAnnouncements/TabId/2329/ArtMID/7730/ArticleID/30136/Emotional-Survival-of-First-Responders.aspx

[10] HELPGUIDE.ORG Coping with Grief and Loss. https://www.michigan.gov/documents/mdcs/griefloss.htm_617933_7.pdf

[11] https://courses.lumenlearning.com/atd-hostos-childdevelopment/chapter/relationships-and-families-in-adulthood/

[12] Bains, Rupinder. "No Right or Wrong Way to Cope with Grief and Loss." The Weekly Review, Alberta Weekly Newspaper Association, 16 Dec. 2014, p. A.3.

[13] Untitled Document [marlenewinell.net]. http://marlenewinell.net/ltf-ch1.html

[14] BREAKTHROUGH| Breaking Through the Barrier | Lies the .... https://www.youtube.com/watch?v=vQCK6nG6LkQ

[15] Zak Funeral Home Cleveland Ohio, Cleveland Ohio Funeral .... https://www.zakfuneralhome.com/grief-and-healing#!

[16] HELPGUIDE.ORG Coping with Grief and Loss. https://www.michigan.gov/documents/mdcs/griefloss.htm_617933_7.pdf

[17] What is grief? - HWS Homepage. https://www.hws.edu/studentlife/pdf/CCSW_Handout_grief.pdf

[18] Healthy You - Grief and Loss. http://des.wa.gov/sites/default/files/public/documents/More%20DOP%20Services/EAP/ISM%20Materials/Healthy-You-Grief-and-Loss.pdf

[19] https://shamansisters.com/blogs/blog/18544775-how-to-perform-a-fire-ceremony

[20] Healing Yourself to Heal Your Child. http://empoweredtoconnect.org/wp-content/uploads/CTC-Chapter-12.pdf

[21] https://www.encyclopedia.com/people/medicine/medicine-biographies/heinz-kohut

[22] http://tinyurl.com/y6a2rdcb

[23] businessresearcher.sagepub.com/sbr-1946-105603-2878495/20180129/the-meditation-industry

24 *Comfortable with Uncertainty,* by Pema Chodron https://books.google.com/
books
id=Vw87euioS0cC&pg=PA150&lpg=PA150&dq=pema+chodron's+"everythin
g+is+workable"&source=bl&ots=SNYPH0uNww&sig=ACfU3U1xwjwpBht4hP
wTobSHSW3BbXjMHA&hl=en&sa=X&ved=2ahUKEwj2iuS8uvgAhVkU98KHV
OHBgIQ6AEwBXoECAQQAQ#v=onepage&q=pema chodron's "everything is
workable"&f=false

25 https://www.theatlantic.com/health/archive/2019/03/buddhism-
meditation-anxiety-therapy/584308

26 Forgive & Forget: Healing the Hurts We Don't Deserve, by Lewis Smedes

27 https://www.academia.edu/36955122/
_Five_Things_Everyone_Should_Know_About_Forgiving_Lewis_Smedes

28 https://www.amazon.com/Art-Forgiving-Lewis-B-Smedes/dp/034541344X

29 https://www.psychologytoday.com/us/blog/fulfillment-any-age/
201108/13-qualities-look-in-effective-psychotherapist

30 https://news.stanford.edu/news/2005/june15/jobs-061505.html

31 http://tinyurl.com/y476qkc6

32 Vicky Beeching, Christian rock star 'I'm gay. God loves me .... https://
www.independent.co.uk/news/people/news/vicky-beeching-star-of-the-
christian-rock-scene-im-gay-god-loves-me-just-the-way-i-am-9667566.html

33 https://www.amazon.com/Undivided-Coming-Becoming-Whole-Living/
dp/0062439901

34 https://www.ted.com/talks/ken_robinson_says_schools_kill_creativity?
language=en

35 20 Celebrities Who Never Finished High School | Fox News. https://
www.foxnews.com/entertainment/20-celebrities-who-never-finished-high-
school

36 Davis, Kortright. "The Legacy of Black Prophetic Moments: Dynastic
Monuments versus Dynamic Movements." Anglican Theological Review, vol.
97, no. 3, Anglican Theological Review, Inc., July 2015, p. 449.

37 https://www.amazon.com/Invisible-Influence-Hidden-Forces-Behavior/dp/
1476759693

[38] Invisible Influence - LIBRIS. https://eastmanchemical.libraryreserve.com/10/50/en/ContentDetails.htm?id=15ACE8FB-9A2E-4AE8-8547-46929BAE7A0F

[39] The Top Five Regrets of the Dying : A Life Transformed by .... https://books.google.com/books/about/The_Top_Five_Regrets_of_the_Dying.html?id=OL8ne9Zgf88C

[40] You may not realize it when it happens, by Walt Disney. http://www.quotes-positive.com/quote/you-not-realize-happens-kick-121/

[41] Google Knows Even More About Your Private Life Than Facebook. https://lifehacker.com/google-knows-even-more-about-you-than-facebook-1825508058

[42] https://www.researchgate.net/publication/23562101_A_history_of_the_early_days_of_personality_testing_in_American_industry_An_obsession_with_adjustment

[43] What the Hell are the Neurons Up To? - authorhouse.com. http://www.authorhouse.com/bookstore/bookdetail.aspx?bookid=SKU-000414691

[44] http://journalpsyche.org/jungian-model-psyche

[45] Carl Jung | Simply Psychology. https://www.simplypsychology.org/carl-jung.html

[46] https://www.simplypsychology.org/carl-jung.html

[47] James Hollis, *Finding Meaning in the Second Half of Life* (Avery, 2005), Kindle loc. 221-223.

[48] The Middle Passage, from Misery to Meaning in Midlife by .... https://appliedjung.com/the-middle-passage/

[49] https://www.amazon.com/Homo-Deus-Brief-History-Tomorrow/dp/0062464345

[50] Palimpsest: A Memoir, Gore Vidal

[51] Complementary Colors - Designbar. https://www.designbaronline.com/complementary_colors/

[52] Before I Die - You Must Know This About The Future .... https://www.youtube.com/watch?v=vsWnynNMCzk

53 https://www.bustle.com/articles/67401-what-were-the-monks-on-house-of-cards-doing-in-the-white-house-they-had-me

54 Songwriters: Kerry Livgren / Kerry A Livgren, *Dust in the Wind* lyrics © Sony/ATV Music Publishing LLC

55 https://www.carl-jung.net/mandala.html

56 http://www.mandalasforthesoul.com/native-american-mandala

57 http://www.cgjungpage.org/learn/articles/culture-and-psyche/908-the-medicine-wheel-as-a-symbol-of-native-american-psychology

58 Anthony Stevens, *Carl Jung: A Very Short Introduction*, (OUP Oxford), Kindle loc: 1793-1795

59 https://www.amazon.com/Red-Book-Philemon-C-Jung/dp/0393065677/ref=sr_1_1?keywords=red+book+jung&qid=1550686002&s=gateway&sr=8-1

60 Carl Jung - Mandala. https://carl-jung.net/mandala.html

61 Symbol - Wikipedia. https://en.wikipedia.org/wiki/Symbology

62 Flower Color Symbolism | Flower Shopping. https://www.flowershopping.com/shop-by-color/FlowerColorSymbolism/

63 Lily Flower Meaning & Symbolism | Teleflora. https://www.teleflora.com/meaning-of-flowers/lily

64 The 3 Steps Of Essentialism: How To Achieve More By Doing https://www.forbes.com/sites/francesbridges/2018/11/29/the-3-steps-of-essentialism-achieving-more-by-doing-less-according-to-greg-mckeown/

65 The Four Aspects of "Self" - Balancing Mind, Body & Soul .... http://www.balancingmindbodysoul.co.uk/spiritual-development/the-four-aspects-of-self

66 The Four Aspects of "Self" - Balancing Mind, Body & Soul .... http://www.balancingmindbodysoul.co.uk/spiritual-development/the-four-aspects-of-self

67 https://www.stjo.org/native-american-culture/native-american-beliefs/four-directions/

68 http://www.businessdictionary.com/definition/psychographics.html, demographics, and ideology.

69 https://www.psychologytoday.com/us/blog/owning-pink/201209/the-health-benefits-finding-your-tribe

70 https://www.ncbi.nlm.nih.gov/pmc/articles/PMC1695733/

71 https://www.census.gov/hhes/migration/about/cal-mig-exp.html

72 Wells, William D. (May 1975). "Psychographics: A critical review". *Journal of Marketing Research*. **12**: 196—213.

73 "Searching for Whitopia". *Richbenjamin.com*. Archived from the original on 1 December 2012. Retrieved 23 March 2013.

74 https://www.newyorker.com/science/maria-konnikova/social-media-affect-math-dunbar-number-friendships

75 https://www.technologyreview.com/s/601369/your-brain-limits-you-to-just-five-bffs

76 http://classics.mit.edu/Aristotle/nicomachaen.html

77 Friendship, Love and Marriage by Henry David Thoreau, https://play.google.com/store/books/details?id=u7KwAAAAIAAJ&rdid=book-u7KwAAAAIAAJ&rdot=1

78 https://www.gutenberg.org/files/1998/1998-h/1998-h.htm

79 http://tinyurl.com/y43467ur

80 http://classics.mit.edu/Aristotle/nicomachaen.8.viii.html

81 https://www.simplypsychology.org/attachment.html

82 https://www.verywellmind.com/john-bowlby-biography-1907-1990-2795514

83 Levine, Amir. Attached: The New Science of Adult Attachment and How It Can Help You Find—and Keep—Love (Kindle Locations 330-337). Penguin Publishing Group. Kindle Edition.

84 https://getrevising.co.uk/revision-notes/continuity_hypothesis_case_study_the_love_quiz

[85] "Attached" by Levine and Heller, Kindle Location 119.

[86] Ibid, Kindle location 163-165.

[87] Ibid, Kindle location 166.

[88] Levine, Amir. Attached: The New Science of Adult Attachment and How It Can Help You Find—and Keep—Love (Kindle Location 634). Penguin Publishing Group. Kindle Edition.

[89] How Toxic People Affect Your Health - HCPNow. https://www.hcpnow.com/how-toxic-people-affect-your-health

[90] Detox Your Relationships | Psychology Today. https://www.psychologytoday.com/us/blog/the-truisms-wellness/201609/detox-your-relationships

[91] http://tinyurl.com/yyvvv6dw

[92] Scalable Learning of Collective Behavior Based on Sparse …. http://www.public.asu.edu/%7Ehuanliu/papers/cikm09.pdf

[93] https://hbr.org/2012/06/learning-charisma-2

[94] How to develop charisma in 3 steps …. https://www.thinkadvisor.com/2011/01/24/advisor-pointer-how-to-develop-charisma-in-3-steps/

[95] https://www.lifehack.org/articles/communication/45-questions-to-ask-to-get-to-know-someone.html

[96] What we Pay Attention to is What we Love. | elephant journal. https://www.elephantjournal.com/2017/09/what-we-pay-attention-to-is-what-we-love

[97] John Muir Quotes (Author of My First Summer in the Sierra …. https://www.goodreads.com/author/quotes/5297.John_Muir?page=5

[98] The Lost Art of Listening by Michael P. Nichols, The Guilford Press; 2 edition (February 16, 2009)

[99] Friend of A Friend by David Burkus, Houghton Mifflin Harcourt, 2018, pp 174-191.

www.ingramcontent.com/pod-product-compliance
Lightning Source LLC
Chambersburg PA
CBHW031151270326
41931CB00006B/232